TOWARDS DIALOGIC TEACHING

Rethinking classroom talk

Fourth edition

Robin Alexander

University of Cambridge

Dialogos

First edition published 2004
Reprinted 2004

Second edition published 2004
Reprinted with revisions 2005 (twice)

Third edition published 2006
Reprinted 2006 (twice), 2007 (twice)

Fourth edition published 2008
Reprinted 2008, 2009, 2010 (twice, with revisions)

Published by Dialogos UK Ltd, YO7 2AP, UK

British Library Cataloguing in Publication Data
A catalogue record for this publication is available from the British Library

ISBN: 978-0-9546943-6-4

To order further copies of this publication, and for information about the author's work and related publications, go to: www.robinalexander.org.uk

CONTENTS

CONTENTS

Introduction

I

INTRODUCTION

In 2001, Blackwell published *Culture and Pedagogy*[1], the account of a research project which over a four-year period took a colleague and myself into schools, classrooms, national ministries, local government offices, teacher training institutions and universities in five countries on three continents. In England, France, India, Russia and the United States we observed and videotaped children and teachers at work; we interviewed school heads, teachers, parents, community leaders, politicians, officials, teacher trainers and researchers; we talked with children; and we collected policy documents, schemes, lesson plans and examples of children's work, adding large numbers of photographs for good measure.

The research was a comparative study. Its principal theme was the way a country's culture and history shape the values and processes of public primary schooling, from the broad sweep of policy down to the day-to-day activities of teachers and children in classrooms. The study also sought to discover what English education might learn to its advantage from comparisons of this kind.

Among the rich array of data which we brought back for analysis, the most exciting was the 130 hours of videotape, all of which was transcribed so that we could revisit and study in different ways the classrooms whose activities we had observed. This material was combined with a further body of recordings from earlier projects, giving us a complete project dataset of 166 lessons from over 100 schools.

As the fieldwork progressed it became increasingly evident that the classroom talk we were hearing and recording was likely to be one of the most potent areas for comparison. Subsequent analysis of the videotapes and transcriptions confirmed this. A culture, after all, is mediated by its language; and it is through language, especially spoken language, that teachers teach and children learn. This was the theme which in its closing pages the book identified as being one of the more promising fruits of its international comparisons; and it was the theme that provoked particular interest among the various official and professional groups with whom the

1   Alexander, R.J. *Culture and Pedagogy: international comparisons in primary education*, Oxford UK and Malden MA: Blackwell 2001. The project (and its follow-up) were largely funded by the Leverhulme Trust.

research was shared once *Culture and Pedagogy* was published: DfES, QCA[2], Ofsted, the National Literacy Strategy, the Primary National Strategy, UKLA[3], and many LEAs.

The dissemination process led to further initiatives. Sponsored by QCA and the National Literacy and Numeracy Strategies (NLNS), three of us started work on a video and print pack which was intended to raise the profile and quality of those kinds of classroom talk which seemed likely to exert the greatest leverage on children's learning and understanding.[4] At the same time, NLNS began to introduce ideas from the research into its training and support materials, and QCA wrote 'dialogic teaching' into its revised guidance on Speaking and Listening, published in November 2003.[5]

Meanwhile, against the background of international achievement studies such as TIMSS, PISA and PIRLS, Ofsted decided to pursue questions raised in *Culture and Pedagogy* about the starting age for formal schooling and the educational experiences of those children who in England are firmly established in their primary education but in many other countries have not yet started school. That led, via further international fieldwork, to the Ofsted report *The Education of Six Year Olds in England, Denmark and Finland*. This study, too, suggested a need to rethink the dynamics and content of classroom interaction.[6]

Next, the team responsible for the government's Primary National Strategy,[7] perhaps in response to criticism that in the Strategy's manifesto, *Excellence and Enjoyment*, oracy was barely mentioned,[8] started to give it

2   Following the QCA dissemination seminar in July 2001 on pedagogical aspects of the *Culture and Pedagogy* research, QCA brought together this work and Ron Carter's research on the grammar of spoken language at a larger conference a year later. The papers appear in QCA (2003) *New Perspectives on Spoken English in the Classroom*, London: QCA.

3   The UKLA paper is Alexander, R.J. (2003) 'Oracy, literacy and pedagogy: international perspectives', in Bearne, E., Dombey, H., Grainger, T. (ed) *Interactions in Language and Literacy in the Classroom*, Milton Keynes: Open University Press, pp 23-35.

4   QCA/DfES *Teaching Through Dialogue*, London: QCA/DfES. This pack was completed in 2002 and still remains unpublished, despite being used by the National Literacy Strategy and the Primary National Strategy (PNS) in their training programmes and conferences since then. Now, at the time of this new edition, it seems probable that the pack will be replaced by something more up to date - for the field is now moving very fast - and will be launched as part of a new PNS initiative. Meanwhile, in November 2005 QCA released a couple of the video clips from the 2002 pack in connection with its *English 21* discussion.

5   QCA/DfES (2003) *Speaking, Listening, Learning: working with children in KS1 and 2*, London: QCA/DfES.

6   Ofsted (2003) *The Education of Six Year Olds in England, Denmark and Finland: an international comparative study*, London: Ofsted. See especially paras 118-137.

7   DfES (2003) *Excellence and Enjoyment: a strategy for primary schools*, London: DfES.

8   Alexander, R.J. (2003) *Still no Pedagogy? Principle, pragmatism and compliance in primary education*, Cambridge: University of Cambridge Faculty of Education (also published in Cambridge Journal of Education 34(1), 2004).

prominence in their training and materials. In doing so, they drew - albeit rather too selectively - on ideas about dialogic teaching presented in previous editions of this publication.

During the same period, I started working with LEAs on their own dialogic teaching initiatives. The first of these, a project involving over 40 schools in North Yorkshire, is now in its fourth year. A similar project started a year later in Barking and Dagenham. In both initiatives, partly in response to the impact of the *Culture and Pedagogy* videos and transcripts, video is being used to support both professional development and project evaluation. Teachers videotape typical lessons at regular intervals during the year and set and review goals relating to the conduct of classroom talk on the basis of their analysis of what they see and hear. The tapes also record the baselines from which each participating teacher, and the LEAs collectively, move forward, and they enable participants to track and evaluate their progress.

These are early days for projects such as those in North Yorkshire and Barking and Dagenham, and while changes in teaching and children's engagement are readily discernible as a result of this kind of intensive video-based intervention, their full impact on children's learning and understanding is still being assessed.[9]

Yet the idea of dialogic teaching is fast catching on. Many local authorities and schools in England, Wales and, latterly, Scotland, have launched initiatives which draw on the ideas in this publication, and there is growing international interest. This is partly because people recognise the potential of dialogic teaching to address an aspect of pedagogy which, considering its importance for children's learning, is surprisingly neglected - in Britain, undoubtedly, but perhaps in a number of other countries too; and partly because it resonates so strongly with evidence from other sources.

Nor, although the work started in the primary sector, is it restricted to primary schools. The take-up from secondary schools increased markedly during 2005, while in more radical vein David Hargreaves and the Specialist Schools and Academies Trust have started exploring the place of dialogic teaching in 'personalised' pedagogies for lifelong learning which centre on student voice, mentoring and assessment for learning.[10] In the policy domain too, think-tanks such as IPPR have started considering the potential of dialogic teaching to address the continuing challenges of social and educational inclusion.

9   Alexander, R.J. (2003) *Talk for Learning: the first year;* Alexander R.J. (2004) *Talk for Learning: the second year,* Northallerton: North Yorkshire County Council; Alexander, R.J. (2005) *Teaching Through Dialogue: the first year,* Barking: London Borough of Barking and Dagenham. See also the final section of this publication.

10   Hargreaves, D.H. (2004 and 2005) *Personalising Learning 2, 3 and 5,* London: Specialist Schools Trust.

In all this, though, evidence must be regarded as paramount. It would be wrong to advocate changes to the culture and conduct of teaching as radical as those discussed here without a secure grounding in evidence from both research and practice; and equally wrong for schools and national agencies to be swept along by a tide which, by failing to engage with the evidence, has more to do with fashion than principle, and whose resulting practice is far from dialogic. This is the sorry trajectory of so many 'new' educational ideas in recent decades and in the end it does a disservice to children no less than to the ideas themselves. Here, then, the publication's many evidential sources are detailed in footnotes, while Section V offers a rather briefer and more selective list of material for further reading and professional support.

The publication ends by arguing that if the dialogic principle is valid for children's learning it may be no less valid for professional learning and school improvement. This is hardly a novel insight, but it may be a necessary corrective to the rampant educational centralisation which Britain – and especially England – has experienced since 1997. For in a centralising culture policy is legitimated by compliance rather than argument and the mantra 'evidence-based-policy' all too often means its opposite – that policy is devised first and its authors then look around, selectively, for evidence to justify it. Both tendencies, of course, are the antithesis of dialogue.

As its title indicates, *Towards Dialogic Teaching* represents work in progress and is not a final statement. This is its fourth edition and fifteenth printing in six years, and what started in 2004 as a short booklet is now not only considerably longer but has generated a sequel which reaches beyond the classroom to examine, within a global framework, pressing questions about curriculum and educational values[11] - not to mention journal articles and book chapters, and a DVD in which teachers and children from the North Yorkshire project begin to enact some of the ideas explored here[12]. Indeed, the field as a whole is moving fast. So, for example, the Economic and Social Research Council (ESRC) funded a seminar programme on 'Dialogue and Development' in mid-2006, while the words 'dialogue' and 'dialogic' appear with increasing frequency in the titles of research proposals.

To help to advance these lines of enquiry, therefore - and of course in the spirit of that dialogue to which all of us in this field are committed - the author would like to hear what readers think about the issues with which this publication deals.[13]

11   Alexander, R.J. (2006) *Education as Dialogue: moral and pedagogical choices for a runaway world*, Hong Kong Institute of Education with Dialogos, now reprinted in extended form in Alexander, R.J. (2008) *Essays on Pedagogy*, Routledge (see this publication, Section V).

12   North Yorkshire County Council (2006) *Talk for Learning: teaching and learning through dialogue* (DVD pack containing text and 24 lesson extracts), North Yorkshire County Council with Dialogos (see p 56).

13   Contact: rja40@cam.ac.uk

II

DIALOGIC TEACHING:
THE CASE AND THE EVIDENCE

Introduction

Talk has always been one of the essential tools of teaching, and the best teachers use it with precision and flair. But talk is much more than an aid to effective teaching. Children, we now know, need to talk, and to experience a rich diet of spoken language, in order to think and to learn. Reading, writing and number may be the acknowledged curriculum 'basics', but talk is arguably the true foundation of learning.

This section sets out the research basis for a kind of teaching in which talk is given the prominence which effective thinking and learning require. It makes the case not for 'speaking and listening' - currently conceived in England's National Curriculum as an aspect of the teaching of English - but for a distinctive pedagogical approach called *dialogic teaching* which reaches across the entire curriculum.

For most of us, talking is easy. We just do it. It is also transitory: unless our talk is taped or transcribed, or has memorable rhetorical, poetic or emotive power, it soon fades to a remembered sensation or vanishes altogether. In contrast the written word is available for endless scrutiny after the event. Indeed, unlike speech there is not one reading 'event' but many, scattered over time and place and mediated by each reader and his or her consciousness and circumstances.

For these and other reasons we may tend to be less reflective about what is said in our classrooms than about what is written. But there is the additional problem, in Britain at least, that considerably lower educational status is ascribed to talk than to writing, and this difference is constantly reinforced. After children have explored ideas through discussion, they are told 'Now write about it.' When their learning and understanding are assessed, it is on the basis of what they have written. When parents or school inspectors look for evidence that children are making progress, it is the written work that they ask to see. Thus an educational culture has evolved in which writing is viewed as the only 'real' school work and as the most reliable medium for measuring pupils' learning.

This emphasis is by no means universal, and one of the important lessons of international research is that it is possible to teach effectively, and indeed to find one's pupils at or near the top of international league tables of pupil achievement, by using teaching in which talk has considerable prominence, and in which talking and writing stand in a different relationship to each other than tends to be the case in Britain.

So whatever other questions we ask when evaluating our teaching, two are fundamental: do we provide and promote the right kind of talk; and how can we strengthen its power to help children think and learn even more effectively than they do?

If established research helps us to answer the first question, recent comparisons between British classrooms and those of other countries throw the second one into sharp relief, for they enable us to view our habitual ideas and practices, as it were, from the outside, and they provide us with different ways to tackle familiar challenges.

What follows was prompted initially by findings from a comparative study of primary education in England, France, India, Russia and the United States which culminated in a detailed analysis of talk from classrooms in these five countries[14]. However, the ideas presented here stem from much more than this one project. My own work in this field started with UK projects in the 1980s.[15] Researchers from several disciplines and countries have long been preoccupied by the place of talk in children's development and education. Most of them recognise that genuine educational advance is achieved less by sensational research findings or headline-grabbing political initiatives than by painstaking effort and enquiry which respect and build on what has gone before. We shall see that cumulation is an important principle in the proper handling of classroom talk. It is also essential to research. Since talking, thinking and knowing are intimately connected, this is no coincidence.

Learning to talk, talking to learn

From the now substantial body of research on language, learning and teaching there are several strands with which we should be particularly concerned.

The first and foremost is psychological. Language and thought are intimately related, and the extent and manner of children's cognitive development depend to a considerable degree on the forms and contexts of language which they have encountered and used. 'When children learn language,' argues Michael Halliday, 'they are not simply engaging in one

---

14   Alexander, R.J. (2001) *Culture and Pedagogy: international comparisons in primary education*, Blackwell, especially pp 391-528.

15   The large-scale evaluation of educational policy, practice and reform in Leeds (1986-91), which included sustained observation and analysis of classroom talk; and the ESRC CICADA study of classroom change and continuity (1990-92), at the core of which was a quantitative analysis of discourse. See: Alexander, R.J. (1995) *Versions of Primary Education*, London: Routledge, chapters 4 and 5.

type of learning among many; rather, they are learning the foundations of learning itself.'[16]

But whereas teaching during the 1960s and 1970s was strongly influenced by the idea - attributed, perhaps unfairly, to Piaget - of the child as a 'lone scientist' who develops cognitively by interacting with stimulating materials, from the 1980s this approach was increasingly challenged by the Vygotskian view that the child's cognitive development also requires it to engage, through the medium of spoken language, with adults, other children and the wider culture.[17] Development, then, is a social process as well as a biological one. Children construct meaning not only from the interplay of what they newly encounter and what they already know, but also from interaction with others. In turn, this interaction is critical not just for children's understanding of the kind of knowledge with which schools deal – mathematics, science and so on – but also for the development of their very identity, their sense of self and worth.

The 'others' with whom children interact assume a critical role in the process of cognitive 'scaffolding', a term first coined by Wood, Bruner and Ross in the 1970s in the context of mother-child interaction and now more commonly applied to what goes on – or does not – in classrooms. This is the use of carefully structured interventions to bridge what Vygotsky called the 'zone of potential (or, in most translations, 'proximal') development', or the gap between the child's existing knowledge and ways of solving problems unaided and the understanding which can be attained only with the guidance of the teacher or a 'more capable peer'.[18]

In other words, learning and development are not synonymous, as in the heyday of progressivism they tended to be regarded. It is true that children learn regardless of the intentions of their parents, carers or teachers, simply by being acutely alive to what is going on around them. But learning *to a specific cultural purpose* requires intervention and support by others. Emphasising the critical role of interaction in this process,

16   Halliday, M.A.K. (1993) 'Towards a language-based theory of learning', *Linguistics in Education*, 5.

17   Bruner, J.S. and Haste. H. (1987) Introduction to *Making Sense: the child's construction of the world*, Routledge; Vygotsky, L.S. (1962) *Thought and Language*, Cambridge MA: M.I.T. Press. Goswami, U. and Bryant, P. (2007) *Children's Cognitive Development and Learning* (Primary Review Research Survey 2/1a), Cambridge: University of Cambridge Faculty of Education.

18   Vygotsky, L.S. (1962) *Mind in Society: the development of higher psychological processes*, Cambridge MA: Harvard University Press; Bruner and Haste, pp 21-2. According to Joan Simon, who was a pioneering translator and disseminator of the work of Vygotsky, Luria, Leontiev and other Russian psychologists, 'Zone of *potential* [or *next*] development' is a more appropriate translation from the Russian than the more usual 'proximal'. See Simon J. (1987) 'Vygotsky and the Vygotskians', *American Journal of Education*, August; also, for one of the most concise of Vygotsky's own accounts of his ideas, Simon, B. and Simon, J. (ed) (1963) *Educational Psychology in the U.S.S.R.* London: Routledge, pp 21-34.

Vygotsky even went as far as to argue that 'the true direction of the development of thinking is not from the individual to the social, but from the social to the individual.'[19]

While it is clear that this approach challenges the once popular view of the teacher as a hands-off 'facilitator', it is important to stress that it does not herald a return to the traditional model of teaching as mere telling or transmitting. Where both of the earlier models implied activity on one side of the teacher-pupil relationship but passivity on the other - active pupils and passive teachers in one, passive pupils and active teachers in the other - the new approach demands both pupil engagement *and* teacher intervention. And the principal means by which pupils actively engage and teachers constructively intervene is through talk.

Such talk, as Daniels emphasises in his recent work on activity theory, must not be regarded as mere 'interaction', narrowly conceived and bounded by the immediacy of the learning task in hand. Classroom talk mediates not just teaching and learning but also the wider culture.[20]

As Bruner again argues, several lines of research – on intersubjectivity, on the nature of the human mind, on metacognition and on collaborative learning – all converge on the principle that children must think for themselves before they truly know and understand, and that teaching must provide them with those linguistic opportunities and encounters which will enable them to do so.[21]

These ideas have been given a further boost by neuroscientific research. It is now understood that talk is necessary not just for learning but also for the building of the brain itself as a physical organism, thereby expanding its power. If, as has long been known, the first three years of life are critical to subsequent development, it is now recognised that the period between 3/4 and 10/11 - the primary phase of schooling, more or less – is one in which the brain in effect restructures itself, building cells, making new fibre connections between cells, pruning old ones, developing the capacity for learning, memory, emotional response and language, all on a scale which decreases markedly thereafter. Between birth and adolescence, brain metabolism is 150 per cent of its adult level, and synaptogenesis (the

19   Vygotsky, L.S. (1962) *Thought and Language,* Cambridge MA: M.I.T. Press, p 10.   On 'scaffolding' see: Bruner, J.S. and Haste, H.E. (ed) (1987) *Making Sense: the child's construction of the world,* London: Routledge, pp 1-25; Wood, D., Bruner, J.S., Ross, G. (1976) 'The role of tutoring in problem-solving' *Journal of Child Psychology and Child Psychiatry,* 17, pp 89-100; Maybin, J., Mercer, N., Stierer, B. (1992) ' "Scaffolding" learning in the classroom', in Norman, K. (ed) *Thinking Voices: the work of the National Oracy Project,* London: Hodder, pp 186-95.

20   Daniels, H. (2001) *Vygotsky and Pedagogy,* London: Routledge/Falmer.

21   Bruner, J.S. (1996) *The Culture of Education,* Cambridge MA: Harvard University Press, pp 56-60.

growth of brain connections) causes the brain's volume to quadruple. Talk actively and vigorously fuels these processes.[22]

Moreover, the periods between birth and 3/4 and between 3/4 and 10/11 are those when the brain's capacity to acquire language is strongest.[23] Apart from underlining the imperative of talk in the home, and in pre-school and primary education, this finding raises a separate question about the way in Britain the learning of foreign languages is postponed until the secondary stage of schooling. By then it may actually be more difficult, not less, to learn a new language. Having said that, brain research also tends to dent the claim that there are all-or-nothing critical periods for learning. Though some kinds of learning are more effective during the early years, synaptogenesis can occur at any period of life and humans retain the capacity to learn, and to learn extensively and in complex domains, throughout their lives.[24]

Neuroscience also supports the Vygotskian critique of teaching as mere developmental facilitation, discussed above. In some domains - perceptual, certainly, and to a degree social too - implicit learning clearly takes place, but higher-order cognitive activities of the kind that characterise formal schooling require both conscious effort and direct intervention. As Goswami notes, responding sceptically to Blakemore and Frith's views on 'learning without awareness':

> Children spend much of their day in classrooms, [but] their brains do not automatically 'notice' how to read or do sums. These skills must be directly taught. It seems much more likely that the power of learning without awareness is relevant to education via social cognition.[25]

These insights from emerging neuroscientific research are doubly helpful: first in confirming the importance of teaching as intervention rather than mere facilitation; secondly, as an endorsement of teaching which capitalises on the collective and interactive environment which classrooms offer. The boundaries may not be precisely delineated: indeed, that's the point, for it seems evident that it is advantageous to the learner if we see implicit social learning and the explicit teaching of higher-order concepts as linked and mutually-supportive processes. In the account of dialogic teaching which we develop in this publication, the dynamics of talk matter no less than its content, while social and cognitive purposes go hand in hand.

22   Johnson, M. (2004) *Developmental Cognitive Neuroscience*, 2nd edition, Oxford: Blackwell.
23   Kotulak, R. (1996) *Inside the Brain: revolutionary discoveries of how the mind works,* Kansas City: Andrews McMeel Publishing.
24   Goswami, U. (2006) 'The brain in the classroom? The state of the art' (Commentary on Blakemore and Frith's *The Learning Brain*), *Developmental Science.* pp 467-9.
25   *Ibid.*

Communicative rights and cognitive challenge

The second strand of research is sociological - or, more specifically, sociolinguistic, for it is concerned with the kinds of language and language environments which classrooms actually provide, as opposed to what the psychological and neuroscientific evidence suggests they ought to provide.

Ever since, during the 1960s, Douglas Barnes explored patterns of teacher-pupil communication in secondary schools[26] and Philip Jackson charted the consequences for children of the unequal relationship of teacher and taught,[27] researchers have been sensitive to the risk that, if we are not careful, classrooms may be places where teachers rather than children do most of the talking; where supposedly open questions are really closed; where instead of thinking through a problem children devote their energies to trying to spot the one 'correct' answer; and where the supposed equality of discussion is subverted by what Tony Edwards calls the 'unequal communicative rights' of a kind of talk which remains stubbornly unlike the talk which takes place anywhere else.[28] Clearly, if classroom talk is to make a meaningful contribution to children's learning and understanding, it must move beyond the acting out of such cognitively restricting rituals.

The third strand of enquiry links to the first two. Following the ORACLE observational research of Galton and Simon during the 1970s and later studies by Mortimore, Alexander, Bennett, Wragg, Pollard and others, we have built up an increasingly comprehensive picture of classroom life, especially in primary schools.[29] Among the features on the debit side which seem particularly resistant to change are the relative scarcity of talk which really challenges children to think for themselves, and especially the low level of cognitive demand in many classroom questions; the continuing prevalence of questions which remain closed despite our claims to be interested in fostering more open forms of enquiry; the habitual and perhaps unthinking use of bland, all-purpose praise rather than feedback of a kind which diagnoses and informs; the seeming paradox of children working everywhere in groups but rarely as groups; the rarity of autonomous pupil-led discussion and problem-solving; and the tendency of classrooms to be places of risk and ambiguity rather than security and

26   Barnes, D., Britton, J., Rosen, H. (1969) *Language, the Learner and the School,* Penguin.
27   Jackson, P.W. (1967) *Life in Classrooms,* New York: Holt, Rinehart and Winston.
28   Edwards, A.D. and Westgate, D.P.G. (1994) *Investigating Classroom Talk,* Falmer.
29   Galton, M., Simon, B. (1980) *Inside the Primary Classroom,* Routledge; Mortimore, P. et al, *School Matters: the Junior Years,* Open Books; Alexander, R.J. (1995) *Versions of Primary Education,* Routledge; Bennett, N. et al (1984) *The Quality of Pupil Learning Experiences,* Lawrence Erlbaum; Wragg, E.C. (1993) *Primary Teaching Skills,* Routledge.

clarity,[30] in which children devise strategies to cope and 'get by' rather than engage.[31]

These findings are mirrored by those from the United States, where the question-answer 'recitation script' remains dominant and - to quote from Nystrand's large-scale study in American middle and high schools - classroom discourse is

> ... overwhelmingly monologic. When teachers were not lecturing, students were either answering questions or completing seatwork. The teacher asked nearly all the questions, few questions were authentic, and few teachers followed up student responses.[32]

'Authentic' questions are those for which the teacher has not prespecified or implied a particular answer. They are contrasted with the much more common 'test' questions in which the teacher retains absolute control over the answers and therefore the direction of the interaction of which individual questions and answers are a part. And crucially for the theme of this publication, Nystrand and his colleagues define 'authentic' questions as dialogic because they 'signal to students the teacher's interest in what they think and know and not just whether they can report what someone else thinks or has said.'[33]

There is also the striking finding from earlier UK research that well-structured oral and collaborative activities maintain children's time on task more consistently than do solitary written and text-based tasks, yet in many classrooms the latter predominate.[34]

Such findings have been filled out by research of a more specifically linguistic kind: for example, by Sinclair and Coulthard on the characteristic 'IRF' exchange of question, response and follow-up,[35] by Dillon on questions, pseudo-questions and the answers they produce,[36] and by Neil Mercer on the repertoire of interactive techniques - recapitulation, elicitation, repetition, reformulation and exhortation - on which teachers daily draw 'for building the future on the foundations of the past'.[37]

These patterns are deeply rooted. The 1990s CICADA and ORACLE II studies showed how the interactive core of primary teaching was largely

30   Galton, M. (1989) *Teaching in the Primary School*, London: Routledge.
31   Pollard, A., Filer, A. (1999) *The Social World of Pupil Career*, London: Cassell.
32   Nystrand, M. with Gamoran, A., Kachy, R. and Prendergast, C. (1997), *Opening Dialogue: understanding the dynamics of language and learning in the English classroom*, New York: Teachers College Press, p 33.
33   *Ibid*, p 38.
34   Alexander, R.J. (1995) *Versions of Primary Education*, London: Routledge, pp 157-8.
35   Sinclair and Coulthard in Coulthard, M. (1992) (ed) *Advances in Spoken Discourse Analysis*, London: Routledge.
36   Dillon, J.T. (1990) *The Practice of Questioning*, London: Routledge.
37   Mercer, N. (2000) *Words and Minds: how we use language to think together*, Routledge.

untouched by the 1980s revolutions in curriculum and assessment.[38] Later studies from Newcastle, Cambridge and Reading universities showed that though the introduction of the UK government's flagship National Literacy and Numeracy Strategies in 1998 and 1999 may have transformed the content and organisation of literacy and numeracy lessons in many English primary schools, they appear to have had much less impact on the deeper layers of classroom talk – especially those habits of questioning and feedback referred to earlier.[39]

Thus, to quote - at some length, but the study merits this - from the investigation by Smith, Hardman, Wall and Mroz into the pedagogical impact of the National Literacy and Numeracy strategies:

> The findings suggest that traditional patterns of whole class interaction have not been dramatically transformed by the Strategies ... In the whole class section of literacy and numeracy lessons, teachers spent the majority of their time either explaining or using highly structured question and answer sequences. Far from encouraging and extending pupil contributions to promote high levels of interaction and cognitive engagement, most of the questions asked were of a low cognitive level designed to funnel pupils' response towards a required answer.[40]

Quantifying these tendencies, the authors go on:

> Open questions made up 10% of the questioning exchanges and 15% of the sample did not ask any such questions. Probing by the teacher, where the teacher stayed with the same child to ask further questions to encourage sustained and extended dialogue, occurred in just over 11% of the questioning exchanges. Uptake questions occurred in only 4% of the teaching exchanges and 43% of the teachers did not use any such moves. Only rarely were teachers' questions used to assist pupils to more complete or elaborated ideas. Most of the pupils' exchanges were very short, with answers lasting on average 5 seconds, and were limited to three words or fewer for 70% of the time.[41]

38   Alexander, R.J., Willcocks, J., Nelson, N. (1996) 'Discourse, pedagogy and the National Curriculum: change and continuity in primary schools', *Research Papers in Education*, 11(1); Galton, M et al (1999) *Inside the Primary Classroom: 20 years on*, Routledge.

39   Hardman, F., Smith, F., Wall, K. (2003) ' "Interactive whole class teaching" in the National Literacy Strategy', *Cambridge Journal of Education*, 33(2), pp 197-215; Moyles, J., Hargreaves, L. *et al* (2003) *Interactive Teaching in the Primary School*, Maidenhead: Open University Press; Skidmore, D. (2002) unpublished paper from ESRC project on *Teacher-Pupil Dialogue and the Comprehension of Literary Texts*.

      Smith, F., Hardman, F, Wall, K., Mroz, M. (2004) 'Interactive whole class teaching in the
40   National Literacy and Numeracy Strategies', *British Educational Research Journal*, 30(3), p 408.

41   *Ibid.*

The recitation script, then, continues to rule, and it is on the deeper layers of teaching and learning talk, and the assumptions by which they are steered, that we most - and most urgently - need to work.

Initiatives and agendas

Yet the past three decades have undoubtedly witnessed a growing belief both that the quality of classroom talk is profoundly important and that its character and context need somehow to be transformed. While Douglas Barnes and his colleagues in the National Association for the Teaching of English were arguing the case which influenced the 1975 Bullock Report's account of oracy and its ideal of 'language across the curriculum',[42] Joan Tough was working with teachers nationwide to develop a more structured approach to the analysis and fostering of children's talk.[43] These initiatives, during the period before the National Curriculum, had a considerable influence on many who were then working in primary and secondary schools.

The National Curriculum itself included speaking and listening as a separate attainment target and defined its parameters in some detail, but talk increasingly gave ground thereafter to the growing pressure of test-led assessment and the unhelpfully narrow concept of literacy which became associated with the 1990s 'standards' drive, especially with the arrival of the Blair government in 1997. 'The job of primary schools' Blair's Education Secretary David Blunkett repeatedly and atavistically intoned, 'is to teach children to read, write and add up.'

'Standards' and politics also contributed to the all-too-brief influence of the National Oracy Project between 1987 and 1993. Coining Andrew Wilkinson's term 'oracy',[44] that project brought together various grassroots initiatives with the aim of fostering and improving talk for learning, and in this it eventually secured the involvement of over half of England's LEAs.[45] In the National Oracy Project, as with a line of work stretching from Barnes's seminal classroom studies of the 1960s to the present, the imprints of Vygotsky and Bruner are very evident, and considerable emphasis is placed on using discussion to empower pupils both as thinkers and as active agents in their own learning.

More recently still, the UK government's Foundation Stage Curriculum Guidance and KS3 Strategy have placed talk centre-stage, and

---

42   Barnes, D., Britton, J., Rosen, H. (1969) *Language, the Learner and the School*, Harmondsworth: Penguin Books; DES (1975) *A Language for Life* (Bullock Report), London: HMSO, especially chapter 10.

43   Tough, J. (1976) *Listening to Children Talking*, London: Ward Lock; Tough, J. (1977) *Talking and Learning: a guide to fostering communication in nursery and infant schools*, London: Ward Lock.

44   Wilkinson, A. (1965) *Spoken English*, Birmingham University Press.

45   Norman, K. (ed) (1992) *Thinking Voices: the work of the National Oracy Project*, Hodder.

the KS1/2 Literacy, Numeracy and Primary Strategies have produced materials encouraging teachers to reflect more deeply on the ways they handle questioning in the context of 'interactive' whole class teaching, on making interaction sustained rather than fragmented during the group stages of these lessons, and on the value of paired and group discussion. The QCA/DfES *Speaking, Listening, Learning* materials, which are being used to support the government's Primary Strategy, go further still, and seek to exploit the 'dialogic' idea which is central to this publication. Regrettably, however, they do so in a way which is tokenistic rather than convinced, still less helpful.

Thus the *Speaking, Listening, Learning* handbook, adopting the usual DfES practice - though no less reprehensible for that - of lifting chunks of text from elsewhere without acknowledgement, quotes this author's definition of dialogic teaching in its glossary, scatters 'dialogue' and 'dialogic' through the text, but takes the idea no further than that.[46] The accompanying book of classroom activities introduces 'ground rules for dialogue' only in Year 4, term 1 (why not earlier?), then offers nothing more until Year 6, term 3, at which point 'techniques of dialogic talk' are exemplified by reference not to dialogue at all, but to 'formal language and spoken standard English.'[47] DfES and QCA, it would seem, have missed the point pretty spectacularly.

Given this latest episode in the sad history of official initiatives in the domain of talk, it would be prudent to be no more than cautious about the prospects of the current renewal of interest. It is not just the preference for appropriating the vocabulary rather than engaging with the ideas. As we see in the next section, public attitudes and the inherited educational culture still militate against the kind of breakthrough which is needed, especially when we compare England with other countries.

What adds urgency to this agenda is that children's access to opportunities for talk outside the school vary considerably, as do the quality and potency of the talk they encounter. The relationship of language, social background and education has been highly contentious ever since Basil Bernstein first explored it in the 1950s, and in today's pluralist society we are properly cautious about allowing cultural difference to be defined as deficit. Yet research continues to identify culturally related differences between children's early linguistic experiences which as clearly disadvantage some children as they empower others.

For example, Hart and Risley show how by the age of four in the United States the child of professional parents will have had nearly twice as many words addressed to it as the working class child, and over four times

---

46   QCA/DfES (2003) *Speaking, Listening, Learning: working with children in KS1 and 2, Handbook,* London: QCA/DfES.
47   QCA/DfES (2003) *Speaking, Listening, Learning: working with children in KS1 and 2, Teaching objectives and classroom activities,* London: QCA/DfES, pp 9 and 11.

as many as the child on welfare. The language experienced is qualitatively different, too: for the middle-class child in the same study, encouragement vastly outweighs discouragement; but for the child on welfare the ratio is reversed and the climate of adult reaction is an overwhelmingly discouraging one.[48]

Such findings remind us that while talk is essential for the intellectual and social development of all children, for some of them the talk which they engage in at school is nothing less than a lifeline.

Learning from other countries

International research show how strikingly different are the status, character, context and uses of talk in many British (and American) classrooms by comparison, especially, with those of some countries in continental Europe[49], where, for example:

- Oracy is regarded as no less important than literacy.
- The relationship between talking, reading and writing is clearly articulated, and talk is seen as intrinsic to literacy, not as separate from it.
- There is a strong tradition of oral pedagogy, with sustained oral work in most lessons, and indeed lessons which are oral from start to finish. This tradition goes back for decades, indeed centuries, and is therefore firmly embedded in the experience and consciousness of children, teachers and parents.
- Across the curriculum as a whole, there is a higher ratio than in British classrooms of oral to text-based learning tasks and activities. In British classrooms, written work tends to be seen as the only 'real' work and oral activity is viewed as a prelude to such work ('now let's write about it') rather than as an end in itself.
- To underline the higher value set on oral activity, some formal assessment may also be oral, not just written.
- The purpose of classroom talk is seen as mainly cognitive, whereas in Britain it tends to be seen as primarily social and affective - about developing children's confidence rather than developing their thinking. The current emphasis on 'communication skills' provides a more instrumental view of talk, but still does not acknowledge its importance in building children's powers to think and reason.

48   Hart, B., Risley, T.R. (1996) *Meaningful Differences in the Everyday Experience of Young American Children*, Brookes Publishing.
49   Alexander, R.J. (2001) *Culture and Pedagogy*, Oxford: Blackwell; Broadfoot, P., Osborn, M., Planel, C., Sharpe, K. (2000) *Promoting Quality in Learning: does England have the answer?* London: Cassell; Reynolds, D., Farrell, S. (1996) Worlds Apart: a review of international surveys of educational achievement involving England, London: Ofsted; Luxton, R.G. (2000) *Interactive Whole Class Teaching: a briefing note,* London: London Borough of Barking and Dagenham; Osborn, M. Broadfoot, P. *et al* (2003) *A World of Difference? Comparing learners across Europe,* Maidenhead: McGraw-Hill.

- Interactions between teachers and individual children are often sustained over a sequence of several question-answer exchanges, whereas in British classrooms, in the interests of maximising participation by as many children as possible, interactions with individuals tend to be briefer, more random and scattered.
- Questions are designed to encourage reasoning and speculation, not just to elicit 'right' answers, and children are given time to think things out, and indeed to think aloud (i.e. 'wait time' or our preferred term 'thinking time'[50]). Consequently, answers in continental classrooms may be more considered and discursive than in their British counterparts.
- 'Wrong' answers are not glossed over, but are treated as stepping-stones to understanding.
- Teacher feedback provides information and diagnosis on which the child can build, rather than judgement alone. Feedback is also more honest: in British (and American) classrooms it is common for a child's contribution to be praised regardless of its appropriateness or quality, so as not to discourage the child. If overused in this way praise soon loses its capacity to do even that. As Black points out, 'feedback given as rewards ... enhances ego – rather than task – involvement.'[51]
- Teaching has pace, but without the clock-watching pressure which has come to be associated with the advocacy of 'pacy' teaching in England by Ofsted and the government's national strategies. This is because many continental teachers seem to understand the difference between mere organisational or interactive pace and *cognitive pace*, or the speed of thinking and learning, which is the product of talk which is extended rather than abbreviated. An emphasis on pace *per se* may actually frustrate understanding rather than promote it.[52]
- Talk tends to display greater attention to discrimination and precision in vocabulary, grammar and syntax, to volume, clarity and expressiveness, and to the development of the distinctive registers required for different subjects and social situations (the oral equivalent of writing genres).[53]

---

50   'Wait time' was coined from Mary Budd Rowe by Courtney Cazden (*Classroom Discourse: the language of teaching and learning*, Heinemann 2001, p 94) and by the Assessment for Learning Group at King's College, London: Black, P., Harrison, C., Lee, C., Marshall, B., Wiliam, D. (2002) *Working Inside the Black Box: assessment for learning in the classroom*, London: King's College School of Education. The problem is that 'wait time' does not tell us what the waiting is for, which is why I prefer 'thinking time'.

51   Ibid, p 19.

52   For a detailed discussion, with examples, of the contrasting principles of *organizational*, *interactive* and *cognitive* pace, see Alexander R.J. (2001) *Culture and Pedagogy*, pp 418-426.

53   Ron Carter of Nottingham University is elucidating the distinctive 'grammar' of talk, with important implications for the teaching of speaking and listening: Carter, R. (2003) 'The grammar of talk: spoken English, grammar and the classroom', in QCA (ed) *New Perspectives on Spoken English in the Classroom*, London: QCA, pp 5-13; QCA (2004) *Introducing the Grammar of Talk*, London: QCA.

This contrasts with the all-purpose informal or 'conversational' style which is more common in Britain and the United States, which may require the use of subject-specific vocabularies (as in the literacy and numeracy strategies) but may make few demands on the child beyond this.

- The culture of classroom talk is more public and confident. Children talk clearly and loudly. They listen and they expect to be listened to. And the making of mistakes in front of other children is intrinsic to learning rather than a matter for shame or embarrassment.
- Other aspects of teaching support talk, not least by securing and maintaining children's attention and time on task. These include: classroom layout and pupil organisation; the structure and sequencing of lessons; the handling of time and pace; the context of routines and rules.
- From the way they themselves use language it is clear that teachers believe that they have a responsibility to model talk at its best.

From interactive whole class teaching to dialogic teaching

If we return to the second of the two questions posed on page 10 ('How can the power of talk to promote and enhance children's learning be strengthened?') we find that the rather different contexts and kinds of classroom talk which can be observed in many countries outside the UK, and which are summarised above, provide some important pointers.

First, though, a cautionary tale about the hazards of international cherry picking. During the 1990s some people used evidence from classrooms in central Europe and the Pacific Rim to press for much more whole class teaching in English schools, believing that it was this practice - and the direct instruction with which it is often (but not inevitably) associated - which was responsible for the high educational standards and spectacular economic growth which these countries achieved.[54]

In fact, direct instruction through whole class teaching is the commonest teaching approach worldwide so it correlates as strongly with low educational standards and low *per capita* GDP as with high. As a way of discovering the magic ingredient x in high educational performance, indeed, this particular correlational exercise is inadmissible. And as if to underline this, the economies of some of the Pacific Rim countries whose pedagogy, we were told, was one of the keys to their prosperity, promptly

---

54   See, for example, Reynolds, D. and Farrell, S. (1996) *Worlds Apart? A review of international surveys of educational achievement involving England*, London: Ofsted; Reynolds, D. *et al* (2002) *World Class Schools: international perspectives on school effectiveness*, London: Routledge Falmer.

crashed. As President Clinton might have said, had he been talking about education rather than the economy, 'It's the culture, stupid.'

Thus, while the corrective was useful at a time when many British teachers still viewed whole class teaching as irredeemably old-fashioned or authoritarian, we need to understand that shifting to whole class teaching of itself guarantees nothing, whether we are concerned with the quality of learning or the quality of classroom talk. The challenge of talk is in fact a generic one: we need to work hard at it in all the contexts in which it is used – whole class, group and individual.

Putting it another way, the *organisational* component of whole class teaching – the teacher talking to the class as a whole – is less significant for children's learning than the *discourse* and *values* with which this organisational arrangement is – or more commonly is not – associated. For whole class teaching can encompass talk which ranges from the exhilarating to the mind-numbingly boring. It can engage and enthuse for life, or it can utterly and permanently alienate, especially when it is supported by those two traditional props to teacher authority, sarcasm and pomposity.[55]

This fundamental caveat about whole class teaching has yet to be fully understood. The editors of a paper I wrote for a QCA publication advocating dialogic teaching introduced it, incorrectly, as an appeal for 'whole class dialogue.' They did the same with a paper by Neil Mercer, much of whose recent work has concentrated not on whole class teaching but on small-group collaborative discussion.[56] 'Interactive whole class teaching' has become, wrongly, the default term. Dialogue, in contrast, can take place in *any* organisational context. It commands attention to the power of talk in teaching and learning wherever it is used.

The problem extends beyond the label to its practical application. In many English primary school classrooms, notwithstanding insistent government advocacy of interactive whole class teaching and national strategies for literacy and numeracy which are costing many millions of pounds of public money, research such as that of Smith, Hardman et al (quoted earlier) shows that the interaction remains stubbornly low-level cognitively and dominated by 'test' questions. Here, then, recitation continues to rule.

No less worryingly, one of the principal criteria of interactive whole class teaching as officially promulgated, that it should 'maintain a good

55   For a critique of the Reynolds and Farrell report, and of the wider advocacy of interactive whole class teaching as educational panacea, see Alexander R.J. (1998) *Other Primary Schools and Ours: hazards of international comparison*, University of Warwick: CREPE.

56   See editorial introductions to the papers by Alexander and Mercer in QCA (2003) *New Perspectives on Spoken English in the Classroom*, London: QCA, pp 3, 26, 64. See also, on small group discussion, Dawes, L., Mercer, N. and Wegerif, R. (2000) *Thinking Together: a programme of activities for developing thinking skills at KS2*, Birmingham: Questions Publishing Co.

pace' and be characterised by 'a sense of urgency, driven by the need to make progress and succeed'[57] appears to be having the opposite effect to that intended. In their EPPI review of studies of the impact of the National Numeracy Strategy, Kyriacou and Goulding report research evidence that 'the increased use of "traditional" whole class teaching with "pace" is in fact undermining the development of a more reflective and strategic approach to thinking about mathematics, and may be creating problems for lower attaining pupils.'[58]

Mindful of these conceptual and practical difficulties, and combining insights from psychology and linguistics with the outcomes of international research,[59] the term 'dialogic teaching' replaces both the vagueness of 'interactive' and the organisational restrictiveness of 'whole class teaching'. It draws our attention away from particular organisational settings to what matters most: the quality, dynamics and content of talk, regardless of the way classrooms and lessons are organised. And it challenges us to re-assess attendant notions of time and pace.

'Dialogic teaching' also resonates with terms used by an increasing number of authorities in the field of language and learning. Jerome Bruner, as we have seen, commends a 'mutualist and dialectical' pedagogy in which 'understanding is fostered through discussion and collaboration'.[60] Gordon Wells uses 'dialogic inquiry' to encapsulate his updating of Vygotsky's ideas for today's classrooms.[61] His idea of teaching as the promoting of a 'community of inquiry' is close to Neil Mercer's use of 'interthinking' to convey the idea that talk in learning is not one-way linear 'communication'

57   DfEE (1999) *The National Numeracy Strategy*, London: DfEE, p 5; DfEE (1998) *The National Literacy Strategy*, London: DfEE, p 8.
58   Kyriacou, C. and Goulding, M. (2004) 'A systematic review of the impact of the Daily Mathematics Lesson in enhancing pupil confidence and competence in early mathematics', in *Research Evidence in Education Library*, London: EPPI, University of London Institute of Education. The reviewers draw here mainly on the work of Denvir and Askew.
59   For relevant international studies see, for example: Stigler, J.W., Hiebert, J. (1999) *The Teaching Gap: best ideas from the world's teachers for improving education in the classroom*, Free Press, NY (Germany, Japan and the United States); Broadfoot, P. et al (2000) *Promoting Quality in Learning: does England have the answer?* Cassell (England and France); Reynolds, D., Farrell, S. (1997) *Worlds Apart? A review of international surveys of educational achievement involving England*, OFSTED (England, Europe, USA and East Asia); Osborn, M. et al (2003) *A World of Difference? Comparing learners across Europe*, Maidenhead: McGraw-Hill (England, Denmark, France); Ofsted (2003) *The Education of Six Year Olds in England, Denmark and Finland*, London: Ofsted; and the work of Burges, Prais, Pepin and Bierhoff on teaching in Hungary, France, Germany and Switzerland. Also, of course, the study which led to the present initiative: Alexander, R.J. (2001) *Culture and Pedagogy*, Blackwell, where the countries were England, France, India, Russia and the United States.
60   Bruner (1996) *op. cit.* p 57.
61   Wells, G. (1999) *Dialogic Inquiry: towards a sociocultural practice and theory of education*, Cambridge University Press.

but a reciprocal process in which ideas are bounced back and forth and on that basis take children's thinking forward.[62]

Reciprocity is also the central principle in Palincsar and Brown's 'reciprocal teaching'. Here, the teacher systematically uses four strategies to structure discussion, work on new material, assess and consolidate understanding, and provide a springboard for development: *questioning* to provoke discussion; *clarifying* to tackle problems in understanding; *summarising* what has been learned so far before discussion moves on; and *predicting* the information which will follow.[63]

Focusing more on the dynamics of interaction, Lindfors shows how in the 'dialogue of enquiry' participants need to accommodate to 'positive and negative politeness', or the way that true dialogue entails challenge and disagreement as well as consensus.[64] Similarly, Douglas Barnes stresses the importance of fostering both the spirit and the procedures of a 'joint enquiry' through which learners can construct shared meanings from the necessarily different frames of reference which each of them brings to the common learning task.[65]

Giving such joint enquiry an incipient political edge, Lauren Resnick coins the term 'accountable talk' to define both the intellectual quality and relational properties of productive talk within communities of learners,[66] an idea also explored by Courtney Cazden[67] - and indeed currently much favoured in the United States, where John Dewey's writings continue to inspire proponents of democratic pedagogy.

Then, confronting the inevitable demand for tests of efficacy, Nystrand *et al* demonstrate empirically how 'dialogic instruction' works its strong positive effect on student achievement.[68] Finally, from Mikhail Bakhtin we pick out the telling axiom that 'if an answer does not give rise to a new question from itself, it falls out of the dialogue'.[69]

Bakhtin's perspective on dialogue is acknowledged by many to be critical to this movement, for he deals not with the mere mechanics of oral communication, but with language in the broadest possible context - in

62   Mercer, N. (2000) *Words and Minds,* Routledge.

63   Brown, A. and Palincsar, A.S. (1989) 'Guided co-operative learning and individual knowledge acquisition,' in L.Resnick, (ed) *Knowing, Learning and Instruction,* Hillsdale NJ: Erlbaum, pp 393-490.

64   Lindfors, J.W. (1999) *Children's Inquiry: using language to make sense of the world,* New York: Teacher's College Press.

65   Barnes, D., Todd, F. (1995) *Communication and Learning Revisited,* Heinemann.

66   Resnick, l.B. (1999) 'Making America smarter', *Education Week Century Series,* 18(40), pp 38-40.

67   Cazden, C.B.(2001) *Classroom Discourse: the language of teaching and learning,* Portsmouth NH: Heinemann, pp 170-2.

68   Nystrand, M., Gamoran, A., Kachur, R., Prendergast, C. *et al* (1997) *Opening Dialogue,* New York: Teachers College Press.

69   Bakhtin, M.M. (1986) *Speech Genres and Other Late Essays,* Austin: University of Texas Press, p 168.

philosophy, science, aesthetics, literary criticism, the novel, history and society. The imperative of dialogue, in Bakhtin's view, pervades all of these.[70] But applied in the more specific contexts of educational discourse and classroom talk, the axiom about questions and answers should give us particular pause for thought. For to Bakhtin dialogue is essential to discourses - to a world - where meanings are neither fixed nor absolute, and where the exchange, acquisition and refinement of meaning is what education is centrally about. Indeed (to link Bakhtin to his compatriot Vygotsky) dialogue is about helping children to locate themselves within the unending conversations of culture and history. With dialogue comes identity.[71]

In the narrower context of that classroom talk through which educational meanings are most characteristically conveyed and explored, dialogue becomes not just a feature of learning but one of its most essential tools. Hence we may need to accept that the child's answer can never be the end of a learning exchange (as in many classrooms it all too readily tends to be) but its true centre of gravity.

Questions, of course are important, and there is no shortage of useful guidance on ways of framing them for different purposes. Thus, questions may recall, elicit, check, probe, instruct, develop or manage. They may be open, closed or leading, narrow or discursive, clear or confused. But important though questions are - and they certainly need to be conceived with care - we could profitably pay no less attention to children's *answers* to our questions and to what we do – or more commonly, alas, fail to do - with those answers. This is why 'uptake' (conversants listening and responding to each other and – especially – teachers following up students' answers) emerges as such a critical factor in the Nystrand process-product study of the relationship between classroom discourse and student learning.[73] And it is why in that study 'authentic' questions and discussion did not invariably promote learning.[74] There's little point in framing a well-conceived question and giving children ample 'wait time' to answer it, if we fail to engage with the answer they give and hence with the understanding or misunderstanding which that answer reveals.[75]

70   Bakhtin, M.M. (1981) *The Dialogic Imagination*, Austin: University of Texas Press; Holquist, M. (1990) *Dialogism: Bakhtin and his world*, London: Routledge.
71   Vygotsky, L.S. (1978) *Mind in Society*, Cambridge MA: Harvard University Press.
72   Dillon, J.T. (1990) *The Practice of Questioning*, London: Routledge; Brown, G. and Wragg, E.C. (1993) *Questioning*, London: Routledge; Mills, K. (1998) *Questions, Answers and Feedback in Primary Teaching*, University of Warwick: CREPE.
73   Nystrand, M. *et al* (1997) *Opening Dialogue*, New York: Teachers College Press, p 39.
74   Nystrand, M. *et al* (1997) *Opening Dialogue*, New York: Teachers College Press, p 72.
75   In Britain, 'wait time' is associated with the work on assessment for learning by Paul Black and his colleagues. In the United States, apart from recent applications by Courtney Cazden, it goes back much further, to the 1970s work of science educator Mary Budd Rowe: Rowe, M.B. (1974) 'Relation of Wait-time and rewards to the development of language, logic and fate control', *Journal of Research in Science Teaching*, 11(2) pp 81-94, and 11(4) pp 291-308. I am grateful to Jonathan Osborne for these two references.

Put another way, if we want children to talk to learn - as well as learn to talk - then what they say probably matters more than what teachers say. So it is the qualities of extension and cumulation which transform classroom talk from the familiar closed question / answer / feedback routine into purposeful and productive dialogue where questions, answers and feedback progressively build into coherent and expanding chains of enquiry and understanding. And, as Carol Feldman argues, thematic continuity and the constant interplay between the familiar and the new are prerequisites for development and growth in thought as well as language.[76]

Neil Mercer has identified five common oral techniques which teachers use to build pupils' new understanding on their past activity:

- *recapitulation:* summarising and reviewing what has gone before;
- *elicitation:* asking a question designed to stimulate recall;
- *repetition:* repeating a pupil's answer, either to give it general prominence or to encourage an alternative;
- *reformulation:* paraphrasing a pupil's response, to make it more accessible to the rest of the class or to improve the way it has been expressed;
- *exhortation:* encouraging pupils to 'think' or 'remember' what has been said or done earlier.[77]

Three of these - elicitation, repetition and reformulation - are common features of question-and-answer recitation teaching, to the extent that unless we are careful they may become formulaic or automatic, and lose their power to stimulate and advance children's thinking. Thus, as Edwards and Mercer note, elicitations may be *cued* – that is, a question may incorporate a clue to its required answer – so heavily that answering questions degenerates into a word-completion ritual.[78] Repetition – like praise ('Excellent! Good girl!') – can become so habitual that it seems more like a verbal tic than a meaningful response. And reformulation may leave children wondering whether their answers are being celebrated, dismissed or charitably salvaged.

No less important in the context of Bakhtin's maxim, of these five techniques only reformulation has potential to take a specific answer or statement forward, assuming that it is indeed used deliberately and unambiguously. Yet on its own it hardly constitutes a dialogic repertoire. It is not sufficient, then, to repeat or reformulate a pupil's contribution: what

76   Feldman, C.F. 'Thought from language: the linguistic construction of cognitive representations', in Bruner, J., Haste, H. (ed) (1987) *Making Sense: the child's construction of the world,* London: Routledge, pp 131-46.

77   Mercer, N. (2000) *Words and Minds: how we use language to think together,* London: Routledge, pp 52-56.

78   Edwards, D. and Mercer, N. (1987) *Common Knowledge: the development of understanding in the classroom,* London: Routledge, pp 142-146.

is said needs actually to be reflected upon, discussed, even argued about, and the dialogic element lies partly in getting pupils themselves to do this. Here the activities which accompany questioning in Palincsar and Brown's 'reciprocal teaching' – clarifying, summarising and predicting – may begin to break the question-answer-repetition mould of recitation.

In a lesson recorded for the unpublished QCA/DfES *Teaching Through Dialogue* pack, there is a sequence in which a primary teacher robustly challenges a child's interpretation of an incident in a story and the child, no less robustly, defends that interpretation, offering clearly articulated arguments in support of her views. This teacher is certainly doing something with children's answers other than merely receiving or orally marking them. Her feedback says not only *what* she thinks about the answer, but *why*. All too often, as the assessment for learning research of Paul Black and his colleagues shows, teachers deliver a judgement on what a child has said or written but do not substantiate or explain it.[79] But in this classroom the exchange doesn't end there, for the teacher also makes it clear that her opinion is just one among many, and that she wants the child to sustain the argument – which this child does.[80]

Some have found this sequence uncomfortably combative, but it captures the essential element of dialectic which distinguishes dialogue from mainstream oral teaching. However, it works only if the classroom culture has moved beyond that one-sided transmissive relationship in which the stock techniques of recitation teaching are traditionally embedded. Without this shift, purportedly dialogic teaching will inhibit and intimidate rather than encourage – even more than standard question-and-answer in fact, because it probes children's thinking and understanding more deeply. But in the sequence in question, the groundwork has clearly been done: the climate is open, yet secure, and the use of humour on both sides underlines this.

One of the ways that the dialogic climate can be fostered is by the negotiation of guiding principles for the handling of talk, which all participants try to respect. Mercer's 'Talk Lessons' programme yielded examples of such principles, or 'talking rules' ('We share our ideas and listen to each other. We talk one at a time. We respect each other's opinions. We give reasons to explain our ideas. If we disagree we ask "Why?" We try to agree at the end').[81] Several of the teachers in the North Yorkshire Talk for

---

79   Black, P. and Wiliam, D. (1998) 'Assessment and classroom learning', *Assessment in Education*, 5(1), pp 7-71.
80   The sequence in question has now been reproduced on a CD from QCA entitled *Opening Up Talk* (2005). It contains just two clips, both of them lifted from the unpublished *Teaching Through Dialogue* pack, and apart from showing this important example manages to open up precious little else, unfortunately.
81   Mercer, N. (2000) *Words and Minds: how we use language to think together*, London: Routledge, pp 161-2.

Learning Project are applying this idea, with evident success, focusing on listening as well as speaking ('We listen carefully. We do not interrupt. We think about what we hear. If we do not understand something we ask').[82] Again, the important feature of these principles is that they apply equally to all: no longer is there one rule for the teacher and another for the pupils. Contrast these with Tony Edwards' list of tacit 'rules of communicative competence' distilled from secondary classrooms in which, for example, the teacher asks questions about lesson content, but pupils may ask questions only about lesson routine or administration; or the teacher may disagree with the child but never *vice versa*.[83]

The essential features of the dialogic classroom are brought together in the five principles which follow, and in the indicators listed in Part III. In a nutshell, then, dialogic teaching is:

- *collective:* teachers and children address learning tasks together, whether as a group or as a class, rather than in isolation;
- *reciprocal:* teachers and children listen to each other, share ideas and consider alternative viewpoints;
- *supportive:* children articulate their ideas freely, without fear of embarrassment over 'wrong' answers; and they help each other to reach common understandings;
- *cumulative:* teachers and children build on their own and each other's ideas and chain them into coherent lines of thinking and enquiry;
- *purposeful:* teachers plan and facilitate dialogic teaching with particular educational goals in view.

We shall have more to say about the practical viability of these principles in section IV.

Extending the teaching repertoire

It has long been customary to reduce the act of teaching to a choice between two basic approaches. These are named, variously, 'formal', 'traditional' or 'didactic' and 'informal', 'non-traditional' 'exploratory' or 'enquiry-based'. Such dualities have been profoundly unhelpful to the development of both effective teaching and the balanced debate on which it depends. By reducing classroom decision-making to an almost Manichaean choice between polar opposites, those responsible have not only given comfort to journalists and politicians who believe that their credibility depends on the successful retailing of such simplistic nonsense; they have also grossly

82 Alexander, R.J. (2003) *Talk for Learning: the first year,* Northallerton: North Yorkshire County Council, p 13.
83 Edwards, A.D. (1992) 'Teacher talk and pupil competence' in K.Norman (ed) *Thinking Voices: the work of the National Oracy Project,* London: Hodder and Stoughton, pp 235-6.

misrepresented the range of pedagogical possibilities which are available to every teacher.

In the so-called 'three wise men' report of 1992 we attempted (with limited success in the over-heated political climate of the time, it must be admitted) to replace such dichotomisation by the notion of *repertoire*, or the principle that the diversity of pupils, classroom conditions and curriculum goals with which a teacher is daily confronted demands an array of organisational strategies and transactional skills rather than a single, set procedure, and that judgements about when and how these should be deployed should be 'educational … rather than doctrinal … The critical notion is that of fitness for purpose.'[84]

We were especially exercised at that time by the debate about individual, group and whole-class teaching, to which the 'fitness for purpose' principle applied in what seemed to us a pretty obvious way, but the same argument applies to classroom talk, where the choice is frequently reduced to 'didactic'/'exploratory' or 'telling'/'discovering'. Now, though, we are helped by recent evidence from international research, which fills out the range of alternatives.[85] So, across the classrooms of the world, we find not two opposing paradigms but six - and there are no doubt others:

- *Teaching as transmission:* inculcating information and skills deemed socially/economically necessary.
- *Teaching as initiation:* giving learners access to the culture's stock of high-status knowledge (mathematics, science, literature, history, the arts etc) and enabling them to use its modes of enquiry and ways of making sense.
- *Teaching as negotiation:* enacting the democratic principle in teaching; seeing knowledge as fluid rather than fixed, created afresh rather than handed down; treating teachers and pupils as joint enquirers.
- *Teaching as facilitation:* respecting and nurturing individual differences; responding to developmental need rather than societal imperatives; and to the pupil's readiness rather than the teacher's timetable; facilitating rather than directing.
- *Teaching as acceleration:* outpacing individual development rather than following it; moving forward collectively towards common goals, bridging the 'natural' and 'cultural' lines of development.
- *Teaching as technique:* focusing on the teaching act rather than its underlying views of knowledge or the learner; emphasising structure, graduated tasks, economy, conciseness and pace in all teaching.[86]

84   Alexander, R.J., Rose, J, Woodhead, C. (1992) *Curriculum Organisation and Classroom Practice in Primary Schools: a discussion paper*, London: DES, paras 99-101.
85   Alexander, R.J. (2002) 'Dichotomous pedagogies and the promise of comparative research', American Educational Research Association, now reprinted (revised) in Alexander, R.J. (2008) *Essays on Pedagogy*, London: Routledge, chapter 4.
86   Alexander, R.J. (2001) *Culture and Pedagogy, Blackwell*, pp 424-5

Transmission and initiation arise from a preoccupation with the knowledge, understanding or skills which are to be acquired, though initiation offers a very different take on knowledge to transmission. Facilitation starts instead with assumptions about the nature of the learner. Negotiation and acceleration represent contrasting standpoints on the relationship between the learner and what is to be learned. Technique remains relatively agnostic on these matters and strives instead for efficiency. For those who care to trace the genealogy of these ideas, the influences of Arnold, Dewey, Piaget, Vygotsky and Comenius are readily detectable.

This typology, which arose from close comparative study of teaching in five very different countries, hints at realms of debate about the relationship between teaching, culture, knowledge and learning for which the tired old 'traditional'/'progressive' distinction is woefully inadequate. Similarly, if we study comparatively the interaction through which teaching is enacted in different countries we encounter first of all a basic repertoire of three kinds of teaching talk:

- *rote* (teacher-class): the drilling of facts, ideas and routines through constant repetition;
- *recitation* (teacher-class or teacher-group): the accumulation of knowledge and understanding through questions designed to test or stimulate recall of what has been previously encountered, or to cue pupils to work out the answer from clues provided in the question;
- *instruction / exposition* (teacher-class, teacher-group or teacher-individual): telling the pupil what to do, and/or imparting information, and/or explaining facts, principles or procedures.

These provide the familiar and traditional bedrock of teaching by direct instruction. Less frequently, but no less universally, we find some teachers also using:

- *discussion* (teacher-class, teacher-group or pupil-pupil): the exchange of ideas with a view to sharing information and solving problems;
- *dialogue* (teacher-class, teacher-group, teacher-individual, or pupil-pupil): achieving common understanding through structured, cumulative questioning and discussion which guide and prompt, reduce choices, minimise risk and error, and expedite 'handover' of concepts and principles.[87]

87 This last definition owes much to Jerome Bruner. See Bruner, J.S. (1978) 'The role of dialogue in language acquisition' in R.Sinclair, A. Jarvella and W.Levelt (eds) *The Child's Conception of Language*, New York: Springer-Verlag; Bruner, J.S. (1995) 'Vygotsky: a historical and cultural perspective', in J.V.Wertsch (ed) (1995) *Culture, Communication and Cognition: Vygotskian Perspectives*, Cambridge: Cambridge University Press; the five versions of teaching talk, above, are first postulated in Alexander, R.J. (2001) *Culture and Pedagogy: international comparisons in primary education*, Oxford: Blackwell, pp 526-7.

Only the last two of these are likely to meet the criteria of dialogic teaching set out earlier, and while we are not arguing that rote should disappear (for even this most elemental form of teaching has its place) we would certainly suggest that teaching which confines itself to the first three kinds of talk - drilling, questioning for recall and telling - is unlikely to offer the kinds of cognitive challenge which children need or which a broad and balanced curriculum requires.

In fact, the evidence summarised in this section indicates that of the five kinds of talk, discussion and scaffolded dialogue have by far the greatest cognitive potential. But they also, without doubt, demand most of teachers' skill and subject knowledge. Rote, recitation and expository teaching give us security. They enable us to remain firmly in control not just of classroom events but also of the ideas with which a lesson deals. They keep power firmly in our hands as teachers. They reduce the risk that the limits of our subject knowledge will be tested, still less exposed. They make it unlikely that awkward questions about evidence, truth and opinion will interrupt the flow of information from teacher to taught. However humanely or humorously packaged, they are monologic. In contrast, dialogic teaching challenges not only children's understanding but also our own. It demands that we have a secure conceptual map of a lesson's subject-matter, and that we give children greater freedom to explore the territory which that map covers.

Yet, and this is no less important for the teacher facing practical choices about what to do, how and when, all five kinds of talk have their place, provided that each is appropriately and sensitively used. As with choices about whole class, group and individual patterns of organisation this is a matter of repertoire and its intelligent and appropriate use. There are times when we may need to use repetition in order to commit a fact, spelling or formula to memory. There are times when a clear and vivid explanation is essential. There are even times when the broad open question ('Now who can tell me...?') or a rapid sequence of cued questioning and competitive bidding may serve to get things going on a cold morning and take us back into yesterday's theme. But if that is all we do, then children will learn and understand far, far less than they could or should. On the basis of the national and international evidence to which we have referred, recitation is and remains the default mode of classroom interaction. In contrast, discussion and dialogue are the rarest yet also the most cognitively potent elements in the basic repertoire of classroom talk.[88]

88   Courtney Cazden's work also supports the idea of *repertoire* in classroom talk (Cazden, C. (2001) *Classroom Discourse: the language of teaching and learning*, Heinemann, especially chapters 3 and 5.

Talking and knowing

So far we have justified dialogic teaching by reference to its claims to advance children's learning, understanding, confidence and engagement. We end this section with four further justifications, all of them, as it happens, prominent in contemporary educational debate.

First, dialogic teaching reflects a view that knowledge and understanding come from testing evidence, analysing ideas and exploring values, rather than unquestioningly accepting somebody else's certainties. This applies in the context of academic subjects, where the stance is essential if knowledge is to develop rather than remain static. But it also applies in everyday life, and indeed without it the principle of lifelong learning may be little more than rhetoric. Transmissive pedagogies are based on a view of knowledge as given, propositional and fixed. Dialogue presupposes a view of knowledge which is more open and processual than this.

During the 1960s cynics pointed out that much 'discovery' learning was nothing of the sort, but was merely a device for cloaking simple transmission teaching in the then fashionable aura of open-ended enquiry. In the same way, the so-called 'Socratic method' seems dialogic but is in fact a device for eliciting, by question and answer, what is already known. There are many situations when teachers, too, will use dialogue to steer children in a particular direction, and in this sense dialogic teaching may not conform strictly to Bakhtin's idea of the unending conversation.

Yet the term 'dialogue' remains legitimate, because instead of simply telling children what they want them to know, teachers are using dialogic means to probe children's understanding, discover the most appropriate springboard for taking this understanding forward, and – to complicate the metaphor – the most suitable bridge (or of course scaffolding) by which that further understanding might be secured. By this process children come to know by their own unique means and in their own unique way what others may well already know, though each of us knows the same things differently; and the dialogic process reminds us that the quest never ends and there is always more to be discovered.

Dialogue and assessment for learning

As has already been hinted, the ideas presented here overlap those advanced by Paul Black and his colleagues in support of a radical shift towards a new dynamic of 'assessment for learning' (a more satisfactory and purposeful term than the rather flabby 'teacher assessment' which it replaced). The King's group argue that many teachers 'do not plan and conduct classroom dialogue in ways that might help pupils to learn' and, like us, stress the importance of carefully-focused questions, 'wait [thinking] time', informative feedback, and a climate of talk which ensures that children participate actively in lessons, 'listen to and respect one another's ideas' and understand 'that learning may depend less on their capacity to spot the right answer and more on their readiness to express and discuss their own understanding.' They offer suggestions for classroom assessment which are remarkably similar to those we advance here for dialogic teaching,[89] to the extent that we might suggest the alternative term 'dialogic assessment'.

The overlap between the concepts of dialogic teaching and assessment for learning is no coincidence. The acts of teaching and assessing are intimately connected. As a means of securing and reinforcing this link, dialogic teaching is economic as well as effective, for at the same time as it engages pupils and advances their learning, it informs the teacher and the pupil precisely how that learning is progressing and what needs to be done to accelerate and consolidate it.

Dialogue and citizenship

The interactive skills which children begin to develop through effective dialogic teaching – listening attentively and responsively to others, framing and asking questions, presenting and evaluating ideas, arguing and justifying points of view – are also among the core skills of citizenship. Citizenship is non-statutory in England until children reach the age of eleven, but they will surely not acquire the 'skills of enquiry and communication, participation and responsible action' which are central to the KS3/4 Citizenship Programme of Study,[90] without an appropriate foundation at KS1 and 2. The skills specified by QCA, needless to say, are not confined to a timetabled slot called 'citizenship', but are generic, and indeed the KS1/2 non-statutory guidelines for personal, social, health education and citizenship have a strongly interactive and indeed dialectical emphasis.[91]

The recent EPPI review of evidence on citizenship education supports my argument here. The EPPI team found that:

> The quality of dialogue and discourse is central to learning in citizenship education ... Dialogue and discourse are connected with

89   Black, P., Wiliam, D. (1998) *Inside the Black Box: raising standards through classroom assessment*, London: King's College School of Education; Black, P., Harrison, C., Lee, C., Marshall, B., Wiliam, D. (2002) *Working Inside the Black Box: assessment for learning in the classroom*, London: King's College School of Education; Black, P., Harrison, C., Lee, C., Marshall, B., Wiliam, D. (2003) *Assessment for Learning: putting it into practice*, Maidenhead: Open University Press.

90   DfES/QCA (1999) *The National Curriculum: handbook for secondary teachers in England*, London: DfES/QCA, pp 184-5.

91   QCA (1999) *The National Curriculum: handbook for primary teachers*, London: QCA, pp 136-141.

learning about shared values, human rights, and issues of justice and equality ... Transformative, dialogical and participatory pedagogies complement and sustain achievement rather than divert attention from it.[92]

Yet - to return to the international comparisons with which this booklet began - these points are perhaps better understood outside the UK than within it. In France, for example, education is deemed a prerequisite for citizenship: mastery of the French language, and the ability to express one's ideas, question the ideas of others, and hold one's own in conversation and argument are unambiguously conditions both of the educated person and the active and responsible citizen.

It is time that talk acquired this sort of status in British education. Only then will we halt the inexorable blunting by cliché, euphemism and flaccidity of our language's probing edge; and only then will those who wield political and financial power be called to account - not by a handful of media stalwarts but by an articulate and vigilant citizenry - for the evasions and lies they routinely substitute for argument.

Dialogue, personalisation and lifelong learning

In 2004 the UK government launched another of its 'big ideas': personalised learning. Indeed, it began to apply the principles of personalisation and choice to an ever-expanding range of public services.

The initial exegesis was characteristically flaccid, and ministers were more able to say what personalised learning was *not* than what it is. So, somewhat tendentiously (and in the process lashing out at the usual 1960s suspects – how convenient and habitual this scapegoating has become), David Miliband asserted that personalised learning was 'not a return to child-centred theories ... about letting pupils learn on their own ... about abandoning the national curriculum ... [or] a license to let pupils coast at their own pace.'[93]

More recently however, David Hargreaves has given personalisation in learning genuine and much-needed substance in a series of pamphlets for the Specialist Schools Trust. In these, he identifies nine 'gateways' to what

92   Deakin Crick, R., Taylor, M., Ritchie, S., Samuel, E., Durant, K. (2005) *A Systematic Review of the impact of Citizenship Education on Student Learning and Achievement*, London: EPPI-Centre, Social Science Research Unit, Institute of Education.

93   Miliband, D. (2004) 'Choice and voice in personalised learning', speech to the DfES/Demos/OECD conference on *Personalising Education: the future of public sector reform*, London, 18 May, pp 3-4. For a critique of personalised learning as initially presented, see Alexander R.J. (2004) 'Excellence, enjoyment and personalised learning: a true foundation for choice?' *Education Review*, 18(1) pp 15-33.

he prefers to call personalising learning. Three of these relate closely to the idea of dialogic teaching. The first is student *voice*, which Hargreaves defines as:

> How students come to play a more active role in their education and schooling as a direct result of teachers becoming more attentive, in sustained or routine ways, to what students say about their experience of learning and of school life. [94]

The role of dialogue in enabling student voice to be accessed and legitimated should by now be evident: being 'attentive to what students say about their experience of learning' is, for the dialogic teacher, the *sine qua non*. Note that the emphasis here is not on what students say about the subject-matter in hand – for that doesn't take us much beyond the conventional focus of classroom interaction - but on how they view the process of engaging with that subject-matter. This stronger sense of 'voice', then, is about empowerment.

The second gateway is *assessment for learning*, whose kinship with dialogic teaching we have also established (see above). The third is *learning to learn*. Admitting the difficulty of giving this hackneyed phrase a precise and viable meaning, Hargreaves ties it to two imperatives: the need for students to acquire skills and dispositions which will enable them to go on learning once they step outside formal educational institutions (lifelong learning) and the psychological desirability of meta-cognition, or 'thinking about one's thinking and learning about one's learning.'[95] Here, too, the potential of dialogue (perhaps, indeed, its necessity) is evident, for dialogic teaching deals not just with what is to be learned but how. It explores the learner's thought processes. It treats students' contributions, and especially their answers to the teacher's questions, as stages in an ongoing cognitive quest rather than as terminal points. And it nurtures the student's engagement, confidence, independence and responsibility – all, as it happens, conditions for the successful personalisation of learning which Hargreaves himself identifies.[96]

The new pedagogical nexus?

It is dangerous, arrogant and foolhardy to claim too much for an idea, however well-grounded in evidence it appears to be. Dialogic teaching is certainly not a panacea, and indeed I have been at pains to stress – and do

94   Hargreaves, D.H. (2004) *Personalising Learning 2: student voice and assessment for learning*, London: Specialist Schools Trust.
95   Hargreaves, D.H. (2005) *Personalising Learning 3: learning to learn and the new technologies*, London: Specialist Schools Trust.
96   Hargreaves, D.H. (2005) *Personalising Learning 5: mentoring and coaching, and workforce development*, London: Specialist Schools Trust.

so again in the next section – that dialogic teaching demands a *repertoire* of teaching skills and techniques, all underpinned by clear educational principles, and that this repertoire probably includes such traditional – and in some quarters despised – procedures as rote, recitation and exposition.

Yet from this brief exploration two conclusions seem justified. First, there is an inexorability in the way the research evidence on language, cognition, learning and pedagogy converge on what we have defined here as dialogic teaching. Second, alongside this pedagogical argument there is a broader educational one: dialogic teaching seems to find a convincing place in the 21st century nexus of citizenship, personalisation and lifelong learning. Each of these is - or, once detached from its surrounding rhetoric, ought to be - about empowerment of the individual: as thinker, as learner and as citizen.

The next step in our journey, then, is to apply these ideas to the curriculum and the goals of education in what could well be the make-or-break century for humankind.[97] It is clear already that a dialogic pedagogy does not sit comfortably with a rigidly canonical - that is to say, monologic - account of knowledge. More than that, though: if individual learners are indeed empowered in the ways I have indicated, and if they begin to exercise that power, then the days of a social order predicated on mass acquiescence in minority power are surely numbered – whether that power is manifested in its familiar guises of wealth, status and political control, or in the unquestioned assumption that certain people, and they alone, have the right to say 'This is the way things are, and this is the way they will be'.

97   I have begun to do so: see the new companion publication to this one, initially written for a Chinese audience but now available from Dialogos: Alexander, R.J. (2006) *Education as Dialogue: moral and pedagogical choices for a runaway world*, Hong Kong Institute of Education/Dialogos. The paper is reprinted, in revised and extended form, in Alexander, R.J. (2008) *Essays on Pedagogy*, London: Routledge.

III

DIALOGIC TEACHING: PRINCIPLES, REPERTOIRES AND INDICATORS

The previous section argued the case for dialogic teaching from educational principle and from national and international evidence. The present section crystallises this case as sets of justifications, principles, repertoires and indicators for classroom use.

Justifications

There are seven arguments for making talk central to an empowering pedagogy:

- *Communicative:* talk is humankind's principal means of communication, especially in an era when children are becoming more familiar with visual images than the written word.
- *Social:* talk builds relationships, confidence and a sense of self.
- *Cultural:* talk creates and sustains individual and collective identities.
- *Neuroscientific:* language, and especially spoken language, builds connections in the brain; during the early and pre-adolescent years pre-eminently so.
- *Psychological:* language and the development of thought are inseparable. Learning is a social process, and high-quality talk helps to scaffold the pupil's understanding from what is currently known to what has yet to be known.
- *Pedagogical:* process and process-product research show that cognitively enriching talk engages pupils' attention and motivation, increases time on task and produces measurable learning gains.
- *Political:* democracies need citizens who can argue, reason, challenge, question, present cases and evaluate them. Democracies decline when citizens listen rather than talk, and when they comply rather than debate.

Principles

Starting from the justifications above, we argue not for more of the same kind of classroom talk that children already encounter, but for a particular kind of interactive experience which we call dialogic teaching. Dialogic teaching harnesses the power of talk to engage children, stimulate and extend their thinking, and advance their learning and understanding. Not all classroom talk secures these outcomes, and some may even discourage them. Dialogic teaching is:

- *collective:* teachers and children address learning tasks together, whether as a group or as a class;
- *reciprocal:* teachers and children listen to each other, share ideas and consider alternative viewpoints;
- *supportive:* children articulate their ideas freely, without fear of embarrassment over 'wrong' answers; and they help each other to reach common understandings;
- *cumulative:* teachers and children build on their own and each other's ideas and chain them into coherent lines of thinking and enquiry;
- *purposeful:* teachers plan and steer classroom talk with specific educational goals in view.

These five principles are by far the most important component of this theory or framework of dialogic teaching. Talk is an idiosyncratic activity, and a mechanistic approach to its development in classrooms is to be avoided. But if in broad terms classroom talk does not meet the five conditions above, whatever form it takes, it is not dialogic.

Repertoires (i): talk for everyday life

We can identify six broad categories of talk to empower and support everyday interaction. Whatever else schools do, they should ensure that children are given ample opportunities to develop and explore each of these:

- *Transactional talk* - to manage a wide range of social encounters and to convey and exchange meaning and intention.
- *Expository talk* - to expound, narrate and explain.
- *Interrogatory talk* - to ask questions of different kinds and in diverse contexts.
- *Exploratory talk* - to explore ideas and probe others' thinking.
- *Expressive talk* - to articulate feelings and personal responses.
- *Evaluative talk* - to deliver opinions and make judgements.

Repertoires: (ii) talk for teaching

Alongside the six kinds of everyday talk above, each of which also has its place in the classroom, we can note that most teaching draws on a rather more limited repertoire of classroom talk:

- *rote* (teacher-class): the drilling of facts, ideas and routines through repetition.

- *recitation* (teacher-class or teacher-group): the accumulation of knowledge and understanding through questions designed to test or stimulate recall of what has been previously encountered, or to cue pupils to work out the answer from clues provided in the question.
- *instruction / exposition* (teacher-class, teacher-group or teacher-individual): telling the pupil what to do, and/or imparting information, and/or explaining facts, principles or procedures.

These provide the familiar and traditional bedrock of teaching by direct instruction. Less universally, some teachers also use:

- *discussion* (teacher-class, teacher-group or pupil-pupil): the exchange of ideas with a view to sharing information and solving problems.
- *dialogue* (teacher-class, teacher-group, teacher-pupil, or pupil-pupil): achieving common understanding through structured and cumulative questioning and discussion which guide and prompt, reduce choices, minimise risk and error, and expedite 'handover' of concepts and principles.

The two groups are not mutually exclusive, and we are not arguing that rote, recitation and exposition should be abandoned. All five have their place. Dialogue, therefore, is part of the larger oral repertoire which is needed in order that schools may meet the diverse objectives of a broad curriculum, and so that children may be empowered both in their learning now and later as adult members of society.

Repertoires: (iii) talk for learning

Alongside expanded repertoires of everyday talk and teaching talk we should work no less assiduously at helping children to develop their repertoire of learning talk. This should enable them to:

- *narrate*
- *explain*
- *instruct*
- *ask different kinds of question*
- *receive, act and build upon answers*
- *analyse and solve problems*
- *speculate and imagine*
- *explore and evaluate ideas*
- *discuss*
- *argue, reason and justify*
- *negotiate*

and, in order that they can do this effectively with others:

- *listen*
- *be receptive to alternative viewpoints*
- *think about what they hear*
- *give others time to think.*

Repertoire (iv): organisational contexts

We have argued against the assumptions embedded in the term 'interactive whole class teaching', for the term itself is a tautology (how can whole class teaching *not* be interactive?) and it is the *quality* of interaction, regardless of organisational context, which matters most. Nevertheless, organisation can shape interactive opportunities and dynamics, so it too should form part of our repertoire. We distinguish five main ways of organising interaction:

- *whole class teaching (teacher and class)*
- *collective group work (teacher led)*
- *collaborative group work (pupil led)*
- *one-to-one (teacher and pupil)*
- *one-to-one (pupil pairs)*

The discursive potential of each of these needs to be thought about carefully in the planning of talk, but all of them provide opportunities for dialogue. Note that there is not one kind of group work but two. The purposes, dynamics and outcomes of group work led by the teacher are very different from group work which is managed by the pupils themselves.

Indicators

The quality of classroom talk depends on many factors: the speaking and listening skills of children and teachers, teachers' subject knowledge (for taking children's thinking forward requires understanding of the directions which that thinking might take), classroom climate, classroom organisation, and so on. The indicators below are placed in two groups. The first group deals with the wider context within which dialogic teaching is placed and the conditions which encourage and support it. The second group lists some of the main properties of the talk which provides the core of dialogic teaching.

It has been suggested the indicators might be coded to show which of the five dialogic teaching principles each of them enacts. Thus, for example, the first three (starting with 'Questions are structured so as to provide thoughtful answers ....') are principally concerned with *cumulation*, though the first one also attends to the need for a *supportive* classroom culture. However, while some – such as 'all parties speak clearly, audibly and expressively' - have a single focus, in this case on the principle of *collectivity*, others – for example, 'children build on their own and each other's contributions' – simultaneously attend to two or more principles, in this case *reciprocity, support and cumulation*.

So the exercise of coding the indicators may actually confuse rather clarify, and for this reason I have left them unadorned. What follows is intended to serve a heuristic purpose, not to be translated into a checklist to which teachers are required to conform. If that were to happen, its dialogic intention would be defeated.

Contexts and conditions

Dialogic teaching is facilitated and supported when:

- different organisational settings and tasks - whole class, collective group, collaborative group, and individual - are deployed to meet different educational goals;
- teachers are prepared to change classroom layout to meet the requirements of different kinds of learning task and different kinds of learning talk;
- to aid concentration, distractions and interruptions are kept to a minimum;
- lesson introductions, transitions and conclusions are economically managed, and care is taken to avoid letting lesson episodes (especially writing tasks) extend beyond (a) the time they require and (b) the children's concentration span;
- lesson introductions and conclusions are long enough to make a difference, and, as far as possible, are concerned with ideas rather than procedures;
- tasks are planned with an eye to their potential to provoke and benefit from talk-based as well as text-based and written activities; and 'now let's talk about it' becomes as familiar as 'now let's write about it';
- time is viewed as a precious resource and there is close attention to time on task;
- teaching demonstrates pace in terms of the cognitive ground it enables pupils to cover, not merely in the speed of its organisation or interaction;
- teachers seek to shift from interactions which are brief and random to those which are longer and more sustained;
- the traditional ratio of written to oral tasks and activities is adjusted to give greater prominence to the latter than hitherto;
- relatedly, more and better use is made of oral assessment, and teachers become as skilled in assessing children's understanding on the basis of what they say as by checking what they write;

- teachers are sensitive to the way their expression, gesture, body language, physical stance and location in the classroom can affect the type and quality of classroom talk;
- teachers work with their pupils to develop: a rich and discriminating vocabulary; the ability to speak confidently, clearly, informatively, expressively and succinctly; the capacity to engage with, and communicate in, different registers and genres; the ability – and will – to listen;
- teachers recognise that in all aspects of classroom talk they themselves are influential models.

Characteristics

Dialogic teaching is indicated by:

- *Teacher-pupil interaction (for example in whole class teaching and teacher-led group work) in which:*
  - questions are structured so as to provoke thoughtful answers, and - no less important -
  - answers provoke further questions and are seen as the building blocks of dialogue rather than its terminal point;
  - individual teacher-pupil and pupil-pupil exchanges are chained into coherent lines of enquiry rather than left stranded and disconnected;
  - there is an appropriate balance between the social and the cognitive purposes of talk, or between encouraging participation and extending understanding;
  - pupils - not just teachers - ask questions and provide explanations, and they are encouraged to do so;
  - turns are managed by shared routines rather than through high-stakes competitive (or reluctant) bidding;
  - those who are not speaking at a given time participate no less actively by listening, looking, reflecting and evaluating, and the classroom is arranged so as to encourage this;
  - all parties speak clearly, audibly and expressively;
  - children understand that different school subjects and social circumstances demand different registers, and they learn how to use them;
  - children have the confidence to make mistakes, and understand that mistakes are viewed as something to learn from rather than be ashamed of;

- *Pupil-pupil interaction (for example, in collaborative group settings) in which:*
  - children listen carefully to each other;
  - they encourage each other to participate and share ideas;
  - they build on their own and each other's contributions;
  - they strive to reach common understanding and agreed conclusions, yet
  - they respect minority viewpoints.

- *Teacher-pupil one-to-one monitoring which:*
  - lasts for long enough to make a difference;
  - is instructional rather than merely supervisory;
  - provides diagnostic feedback on which children can build.

- *Questioning (whether in whole class, group or individual interactions) which:*
  - is anchored in the context and content of the lesson;
  - builds on previous knowledge;
  - elicits evidence of children's understanding;
  - appropriately combines invitations for closed / narrow and open / discursive / speculative responses (what is?' and 'what might be?' questions);
  - combines the routine and the probing;
  - uses cued elicitations and leading questions sparingly rather than habitually;
  - prompts and challenges thinking and reasoning;
  - balances open-endedness with guidance and structure in order to reduce the possibility for error;
  - achieves consistency between form and intent (e.g. where questions are questions rather than instructions, and open questions are genuinely open, rather than invitations to guess the one 'right' answer);
  - gives children time to think.

- *Responses to questioning which:*
  - address the question in the depth it invites rather than worry about spotting the 'correct' answer;
  - move beyond yes/no or simple recall to extended answers involving reasoning, hypothesising and 'thinking aloud';
  - are, where appropriate, considered and discursive rather than brief and prematurely curtailed.

- *Feedback on responses which:*
  - replaces the simple positive, negative or non-committal judgement, or mere repetition of the respondent's answer, by informative diagnostic feedback on which pupils can build;
  - uses reformulation in a way which avoids ambiguity about whether the reformulation signals approval or disapproval;
  - uses praise discriminatingly and appropriately, and filters out the habitual or phatic 'good boy', 'good girl', 'very good', 'excellent', 'fantastic', 'brilliant' etc;
  - keeps lines of enquiry open rather than closes them down;
  - encourages children to articulate their ideas openly and confidently, without fear of embarrassment or retribution if they are wrong.

- *Pupil talk through which children:*
  - narrate
  - explain
  - instruct
  - ask different kinds of question
  - receive, act and build upon answers
  - analyse and solve problems
  - speculate and imagine
  - explore and evaluate ideas
  - discuss
  - argue, reason and justify
  - negotiate.

IV

INTO PRACTICE

Evidence from the classroom

We have referred to a number of major British and American process and process-product research studies which empirically sustain this publication's analysis of the weaknesses of traditional forms of classroom interaction and its arguments for a more dialogic approach. Now, however, evidence is emerging which relates even more directly to what is advocated.

At the time of writing, teachers in primary schools in North Yorkshire are in the fourth year of a dialogic teaching project in which they use video to analyse the quality of their classroom talk, to identify its strengths and weaknesses, to set goals for their professional development, and to enable progress – their own and that of the project as a whole – to be monitored. A similar project is in its second year in the London Borough of Barking and Dagenham, where secondary as well as primary schools are involved. In both projects the dialogic teaching principles, repertoires and indicators in the previous section are being used to frame and assess changes in patterns of classroom interaction and hence learning.

Both projects are being evaluated formatively using observation, interview, video analysis and test data. Together the procedures provide evidence on changes in teaching, pupil engagement and pupil learning. The observational data track changes in all three areas, and the national test data add a further dimension to the evaluation of the impact of dialogic teaching on learning, focusing on measurable outcomes. Additional opportunistic data is available from Ofsted inspection reports.

By the end of the North Yorkshire project's first year there was evidence of the following changes:

- There was more talking about talk, by children as well as teachers.
- Teachers and children were negotiating and observing ground rules which facilitated more effective speaking and listening.
- Teachers were making their questions more focused yet more genuinely open than hitherto, and were reducing their reliance on questions which lead, prompt or heavily cue a specific response.

- There was a discernible shift in questioning strategies away from competitive hands-up *bidding* to the *nominating* of particular children.
- Questions were being formulated more with these children's individual capacities in mind so as to maximise their potential to scaffold understanding from teacher to taught.
- Teachers were giving children more thinking time, and were reducing pressure on them to provide instant responses.
- Children were answering more loudly, clearly and confidently, and at greater length.
- Children were speculating, thinking aloud and helping each other, rather than competing to spot the 'right' answer.
- In receiving children's answers, teachers were avoiding over-use of the stock responses of repetition and reformulation.
- Teachers and children were beginning to build on questions and answers, adopting a questioning strategy of extension (staying with one child or theme) rather than rotation (questioning round the class).
- In discussion, children were listening more carefully and respectfully to each other, and were talking collectively to a common end rather than at or past each other.
- There was greater involvement of less able children, who were finding that the changed dynamics of classroom talk provided them with alternative opportunities to show competence and progress, and of those previously quiet, compliant children 'in the middle' who are often inhibited by unfocused questioning, the competitiveness of bidding and the dominance of some of their peers. The classroom culture in these schools was becoming more inclusive.
- The reading and writing of all children, especially the less able, was benefiting from the greater emphasis on talk, thus confirming that the traditional English idea of literacy without oracy makes little sense. Frequently, this gain was most strikingly noted in the context of lessons in which the proportion of time spent on oral and written tasks was modified somewhat in favour of the former.[98]

Similar changes were discernible in some of the Barking and Dagenham classrooms. There, the following changes were noted:

- Teachers were making more use of questions which probed and/or encouraged analysis and speculation.
- Hands-up bidding was being used more discriminatingly.
- Pupil-teacher exchanges were becoming longer.

98 Alexander, R.J. (2003) *Talk for Learning: the first year,* Northallerton: North Yorkshire County Council.

- Pupil answers were less likely to be merely repeated, and more likely to be commented or built upon.
- There was a shift from directing and controlling discussion to prompting and facilitating it.
- More use was being made of paired talk to prepare for whole class discussion.
- There was a more flexible mix of different kinds of talk – recitation, exposition, discussion, dialogue.
- Information and opinion – rather than yet more questions – were being used to take pupils' thinking forward.
- Pupils were showing a growing confidence in oral pedagogy: more were speaking readily, clearly and audibly.
- Pupils were offering longer responses to teacher questions.
- There was an increase in pupil contributions of an expository, explanatory, justificatory or speculative kind.
- There was more pupil-pupil talk.
- More pupils were taking the initiative and commenting or asking their own questions.[99]

The persistence of recitation

These are important gains, and they provide encouraging evidence that though the changes advocated in this publication are challenging they are also achievable. Yet the long history of planned educational innovation warns us that we should not be carried away by such early signs of success, quite apart from the provisionality of some of the findings, especially in respect of outcomes.

Thus, although in the North Yorkshire project there are discernible shifts in the pattern of KS2 test scores, it is in truth far too early to judge whether these relate to teachers' attempts to make their teaching more dialogic or to factors which may have little or nothing to do with this initiative.

Further, for every classroom where video and observation provide evidence of genuine change in the dynamics and content of talk, there are others in both projects where change is slight or, more commonly, partial. In particular, the sheer staying power of recitation as the default mode of British and American pedagogy has become very apparent, and the video data demonstrate this unflinchingly. It takes little for 'test' questions to re-assert their historic dominance and for feedback to regress to the phatic or uninformative. In this matter, it is important to think beyond the introduction of devices like extended thinking time and nomination, helpful

99 Alexander, R.J. (2004) *The Teaching Through Dialogue Initiative: Year 1*, Barking: London Borough of Barking and Dagenham.

though these are in the facilitation of dialogue, for just as whole class teaching does not guarantee improved standards, so these dialogic devices do not guarantee dialogic outcomes, still less the quality of thinking which dialogue aims to generate. A long answer is not enough: it's what happens to the answer that makes it worth uttering.

In both LEAs therefore, the sustained efforts of the teachers, advisers and inspectors involved are exposing the real challenges of dialogic teaching, and are shedding some light on that persistent research finding we considered earlier – that change in classroom talk may be more apparent than real.

Dilemmas, not deficits

It may be helpful to express these challenges not as deficits to be rectified - hardly an encouraging response to a teacher who conscientiously seeks to transform his or her practice - but as dilemmas to be made explicit, discussed and resolved as part of the normal day-to-day process of professional consultation and development.[100] Thus, the North Yorkshire project evaluation has identified the following dilemmas of dialogic teaching on which, during the project's third year, some of the schools involved have begun to work. These arise directly from teachers' experience of applying the dialogic teaching principles.

Below, the dilemmas are arranged hierarchically: the first two are straightforwardly organisational; the next four relate to ways of changing the conventional character of IRF question-answer-feedback exchanges and of handling discussion. The last three are altogether tougher.

- *Group discussion in a whole class context.* What is the best way of organising the rest of the class when we wish to promote concentrated and productive discussion in one or two groups, with the minimum of distraction?

- *Conditions for whole class dialogue.* Carpet and circle time are valuable, but do they always provide the best conditions for genuine whole-class discussion and dialogue? Should the teacher always be seated on a chair above the children? What message does this convey? Should the children face the teacher rather than each other? What are the best conditions for whole class dialogue?

---

100 See the classic study by Berlak H. and Berlak A. (1981) *Dilemmas of Schooling: teaching and social change,* London: Methuen; and the chapter 'Garden or jungle?' in Alexander, R.J. (1995) *Versions of Primary Education,* London: Routledge.

- *Bidding and nomination.* Dialogic teaching encourages us to reduce the dominance of 'Now who can tell me...?' questions followed by bidding, and to use more focused questions linked to the nomination of specific children. But bidding may still have a place. So what is the right balance of bidding and nomination, and how is each of them best used?

- *Questioning and telling.* Dialogic teaching requires the extension and appropriate use of a broad repertoire of different kinds of teaching talk, yet questions from the teacher remain far and away the most dominant form of teacher talk. Why is this? And what, in the promotion of children's understanding, is the right balance of questioning and exposition? When should we question and when should we tell, inform or explain?

- *Meaningful feedback.* Dialogic teaching aims to replace habitual praise by feedback which informs and extends as well as encourages. What is the best way to achieve this? And is there still a place for praise on its own? If so, when? What is the ideal proportion of each kind of feedback?

- *Making discussion purposeful.* It's all very well to provoke a lively and extended discussion, but should we not also ask where it leads? How and at what point do we pull the threads together and synthesise the understanding achieved in teacher-led discussion? How can we enable the children themselves to do this in group discussion which we do not lead?

- *Learning talk and teaching talk.* In the achievement of understanding, what the child says matters at least as much as what the teacher says. So how can we best develop, alongside our own teaching repertoire, the children's repertoire of learning talk?

- *Is extended talk dialogic teaching?* In project schools there's undoubtedly more thinking time, and children's answers and other contributions are becoming longer, but do these necessarily add up to dialogue? What is the essential difference between extended talk and dialogic talk?

- *Form and content.* In terms of the five principles or criteria of dialogic teaching, how can we best ensure that classroom talk is cumulative and purposeful as well as collective, reciprocal and supportive? What does the teacher need (a) to know, (b) to plan and (c) to do and say in order to make dialogue genuinely cumulative and purposeful?[101]

101   Alexander, R.J. (2005) *Evaluation of the Talk for Learning Project: the second year*, Northallerton: North Yorkshire County Council, pp 25-6.

Form and content

The last of these dilemmas requires further comment, for it comes to the heart of the challenge of transforming talk from recitation into dialogue.

The first three principles of dialogic teaching (collectivity, reciprocity and support) are essentially concerned with the *conduct* and *ethos* of classroom talk. The other two (cumulation and purposefulness) are concerned no less with its *content*. Working with teachers in these two very different regions of Britain has shown that we can dramatically change the dynamics and ethos of classroom talk by making it more collective, reciprocal and supportive, and by setting out 'rules for speaking and listening' which translate these principles into guidelines which children will understand and identify with.

This shift has been achieved in many of the Yorkshire and London project classrooms. The transformation of the classroom culture and the growth in children's confidence are palpable and impressive. It is this which has persuaded so many that everything has changed, for in a sense it has. But if the talk engages yet leads nowhere, its appeal will soon diminish. The critical question concerns the impact of talk on learning, and this is why the other two criteria are so important. We must know where the talk is going, and do what is required to lead it there. That requires us to have a clear sense of purpose and a firm grasp of the content to be covered so that talk is indeed cumulative rather than merely extended. How do we achieve this, and what does it require of us?

Cumulation is possibly the toughest of the five principles of dialogic teaching. Collectivity, reciprocity and support require us to rethink classroom organisation and dynamics, and the unspoken assumptions about the relationship of teacher and taught which inform them. That, for many, is demanding enough. But cumulation makes conceptual as well as attitudinal inroads on professional consciousness and habit. It is rooted no less in the structure and sequencing of subject matter. It requires a conceptual map of what is to be taught, the ability to think laterally within and beyond that map, and an appreciation of where children are 'at' cognitively and what kind of intervention will scaffold their thinking from present to desired understanding.

Cumulation simultaneously makes demands on the teacher's professional skill, subject knowledge, and insight into the capacities and current understanding of each of his/her pupils. Compounding the challenge, cumulation also tests the teacher's ability to receive and review what has been said and to judge what to offer by way of an individually-tailored response which will take learners' thinking forward.

Conventionally, all this must be done in the space of a second or so. But teachers, we might suggest, need thinking time, too. Indeed, it would be refreshing occasionally to hear them say 'I need to think about that answer' rather than that they should feel obliged always to pounce on a pupil's contribution with an instant evaluation or follow-up question. This in turn would signal to pupils that what they say really matters and that answers, too, should arise from careful thought. Cumulative dialogue requires reflection on both sides and, therefore, a re-assessment of the much-vaunted imperative of 'pace'.

Of course, when factual recall is explicitly being tested then the instant correct answer is a wholly legitimate pursuit, but teaching is, or ought to be, about more than this. Questions designed to put the respondent on the spot, answers designed to defeat the interviewer or evade the issue, the event judged as a contest and for good measure conducted against the clock: the power tennis of a political interview does not offer an appropriate model for human learning. Yet it is not that far removed from traditional versions of classroom communicative competence.

These lessons from our own evaluations resonate with a key finding from one of the American studies referred to earlier. Nystrand *et al* report:

> The results of our study suggest that authentic questions, discussion, small-group work ... do not categorically produce learning; indeed we observed many classrooms where this was not the case. We also found that recitation is not categorically ineffective: rather, its effectiveness depends on whether and how teachers expand IRE [initiation-response-evaluation] sequences. The underlying epistemology of classroom interaction defines the bottom line for learning. What ultimately counts is *the extent to which instruction requires students to think, not just report someone else's thinking* ... The dialogicality of instruction [cannot] be judged in terms of the *how* of instruction – question/answer sequences evidenced in face-to-face interaction – alone ... The *what* of instruction – the content and subject-matter – is critical to learning as well.[102]

Of all the dilemmas of dialogic teaching, therefore, we suggest that the ultimate one is how to achieve the perfect marriage of pedagogical form and content. In this matter, teachers may not be helped by the tendency of some researchers to ignore one of the two parties to this potentially happy union. Thus, as Mortimer and Scott note in their study of interaction in secondary science teaching (which offers an important corrective to the tendencies which they criticise in other research): '...the analyses are carried out, and

102   Nystrand, M. et al (1997) *Opening Dialogue,* New York: Teachers College Press, pp 72 and 73. The italics are the authors' own.

the findings reported, solely in terms of patterns of interaction, and the actual content of what is being taught and learned is not regarded as being a significant feature.'[103] Cazden recently voiced a similar concern before looking closely at the kinds of talk required for pursuing different objectives in mathematics teaching: 'There is too little research showing which educational objectives require more dialogic forms of discourse, and which do not.'[104] This is why the notion of *pedagogical repertoire*, which we explored earlier, and which underpins the indicators listed in chapter 4, is a precondition to the successful application of the ideas contained in this publication. Dialogue is not a panacea.

These early insights from the formative evaluation of two dialogic teaching projects suggest that although the five principles are to be viewed as a package, it is helpful to teacher development and support to divide them into two groups. If we want to make the transformation a manageable one, we might concentrate first on getting the ethos and dynamics right, that is, making talk collective, reciprocal and supportive. In those classrooms where these conditions and qualities are established, we can attend much more to the other two principles. Here, we can identify the purposes of the talk and use cumulation to steer it towards those purposes. We can work on listening to and building on answers and getting children to do the same. We can reflect on the feedback we provide. We can re-asses the balance of drawing out (questioning) and putting in (exposition). We can consider how ideas can not merely be *exchanged* in an encouraging and supportive climate but also *built upon*.

Lee Resnick's 'accountable talk' also squares the circle of pedagogical form and epistemic content. She identifies three criteria of accountable talk:

Accountability to knowledge: Participants make use of specific and accurate knowledge ... provide evidence for claims and arguments ... recognise the knowledge or framework required to address a topic.
Accountability to standards of reasoning: Participants use rational strategies to present arguments and draw conclusions ... [and] challenge the quality of each other's reasoning.
Accountability to the learning community: Participants are engaged in talk ... listen attentively to each other ... [and] ask each other questions aimed at clarifying or expanding a proposition.[105]

103 Mortimer, E.F. and Scott, P.H. (2003) *Meaning Making in Secondary Science Classrooms*, Buckingham: Open University Press, p 101.

104 Cazden, C.B. (2005) 'The value of eclecticism in educational reform, 1965-2005', Montreal: AERA 2005 Annual Meeting.

105 Quoted and discussed in Cazden, C.B. (2001) *Classroom Discourse: the language of teaching and learning* (second edition), Portsmouth NH: Heinemann, pp 170-2. See also: Resnick, L.B. (1999) 'Making America Smarter, *Education Week Century Series* 18(40), pp 38-40 and various papers from the University of Pittsburgh Learning Research and Development Center.

Perhaps Resnick draws the net a shade too tightly round those knowledge paradigms which are on the logico-scientific side of the curriculum, and takes too little account of more open and exploratory ways of enquiring and knowing. Nevertheless, the important point which her idea of 'accountable talk' establishes is that classrooms are learning communities, and that the shared conventions by which their conduct is guided make talking, thinking and knowing interdependent. Resnick's criteria for accountable talk take the commonsense 'rules for speaking and listening' which appear in many of our project classrooms beyond the *form* of talk to the handling of its *content*.

Postscript: the indivisibility of learning through dialogue

The dialogic principle, we noted earlier, is all-pervasive. If it is valid for children's learning, it is no less valid for the learning of adults, including teachers. This publication is concerned with classroom learning only, but it is pertinent to invite readers to consider what the dialogic idea might imply for *professional* learning and development. Thus, when professionals talk, plan and work together, how effective are they? Do they listen to each other without interruption? Do they respect each other's viewpoint or do they pontificate, presuming that wisdom comes only with status? Do they accept the discipline of collective problem solving or prefer to pursue private agendas? Do they stick to the topic in hand or do they digress? Yet do they feel able to speculate without fear that their contribution will be sidelined as 'theoretical' or 'irrelevant'? In respect of ideas which have been offered do they ask probing questions, or do they merely hear them and pass on? In respect of what is novel or unfamiliar are they prepared willingly to suspend disbelief? Do discussions take thinking forward or do they go round in circles? Do participants have the skills which all this requires?

Now clearly the contexts and imperatives of child and professional learning are different, as are the relationships of those involved. Nevertheless, we might suggest that the current advocacy of the 'learning school' or 'learning community' imposes a certain responsibility for the advocates to consider what such learning might entail, rather than merely peddle labels. Similarly, moves towards 'distributed' or 'democratic' forms of leadership ('we are all leaders now') imply alternative forms of professional discourse, not merely changes in professional structure and role.

We might also suggest that to commend dialogic learning for the classroom but not the staffroom is likely to be counterproductive as well as inconsistent. The dialogic principle is more effectively promoted if it is also exemplified.

The inconsistency becomes altogether more serious when – as now seems to be happening – a government takes an idea like dialogic teaching and incorporates it none too appropriately into materials for teachers which are prescriptive in intent if not in their rhetoric.[106] Dialogue is indivisible; good practice, as I argued some years ago, is achieved dialectically, not by decree.[107]

The inconsistency descends into darker irony when we recall that one of the justifications for dialogic teaching proposed in the previous section derives from that most basic of political claims, that democracies need citizens who can argue, reason, challenge, question, present cases and evaluate them; and that democracies decline when citizens listen rather than talk, and when they comply rather than debate. True democracy subverts authoritarian tendencies. Perhaps this, rather than a careless misreading of the literature, is why advisers to a centralising and controlling government have reduced dialogue to 'using formal language and spoken standard English'.[108] If so, then little has changed, for it was fear of the socially subversive power of talk which confined it to rote and recitation in those Victorian elementary schools from which today's state schools have descended.

106 At several points in the two DfES/QCA (2003) booklets *Speaking, Listening, Learning: working with children in Key Stages 1 and 2*, London: DFES.

107 Alexander, R.J. (1997) *Policy and Practice in Primary Education: local initiative, national agenda*, London: Routledge, p 287.

108 DfES/QCA (2003) *Speaking, Listening, Learning: working with children in Key Stages 1 and 2. Teaching objectives and classroom activities*, London: DfES, p 11.

V

SUPPORT MATERIALS
AND FURTHER READING

The 100 or so references in earlier sections have been placed in footnotes so as to avoid overbalancing the text with a daunting final bibliography. Those with research interests in language in education or in pedagogy, and those professionals – teachers, inspectors, teacher trainers – who bear formal responsibilities for the quality of teaching, may wish to follow up some of these footnoted sources. Teachers who do not share such specialist concerns may prefer to access the material listed below.

Yet although we concentrate here on professional support through the *Talk for Learning* DVD and other listed materials, we also include a 'wider perspectives' selection which delves more deeply into the linguistic, psychological, cultural and pedagogical bases of the ideas discussed here. Dialogic teaching has an extensive theoretical and empirical genealogy, and - contrary to the message of some of the support material from DCSF and the National Strategies, which in any case tend to use the terms 'dialogue' and 'dialogic' rather loosely, often signifying little more than extended recitation - its advancement cannot be based on classroom tips and research digests alone. For tips and digests may encourage people to apply the ideas without engaging with them, thus subverting the very principle - learning as dialogue - which they purport to advance.

In this edition we have added a section which lists relevant publications from the Cambridge Primary Review, the most comprehensive enquiry into English primary education since the 1960s. .

Support materials

Alexander, R.J. (2005) *Talking to Learn: oracy revisited*, in Conner, C. (ed) *Teaching Texts*, Nottingham, NCSL, pp 75-93.

Black, P., Harrison, C., Lee, C., Marshall, B., Wiliam, D. (2003) *Working Inside the Black Box: assessment for learning in the classroom*, London: King's College School of Education.

Brown, G., Wragg, E.C. (1993) *Questioning*, London: Routledge.

Dawes, L., Mercer, N., Wegerif, R. (2000) *Thinking Together: a programme of activities for developing speaking, listening and thinking skills for children aged 8-11*, Birmingham: Imaginative Minds.

Dawes, L., Sams, C. (2003) *Talk Box: speaking and listening activities for learning at Key Stage 1*, London: David Fulton.

Department for Children, Schools and Families (2007) *Teaching Speaking and Listening* (Secondary National Strategy CD with video clips and transcripts), London: DCSF.

Mills, K. (1998) *Questions, Answers and Feedback in Primary Teaching*, Warwick: University of Warwick Centre for Research in Elementary and Primary Education.

North Yorkshire County Council (2006) *Talk for Learning: teaching and learning through dialogue* (DVD pack containing text and 24 teaching extracts). See box.

Building on *Towards Dialogic Teaching*: linked CD/DVD pack

North Yorkshire County Council (April 2006) *Talk for Learning: teaching and learning through dialogue* (DVD containing 'Dialogic Teaching Essentials' text and 24 filmed classroom extracts from schools involved in the Talk for Learning Project). The DVD is scripted by Robin Alexander and published by North Yorkshire County Council in collaboration with Dialogos. Order from: Mike Smit, North Yorkshire County Council, Selby Area Education Office, 2 Abbey Yard, Selby, North Yorkshire, YO8 4PS, or email mike.smit@northyorks.gov.uk.

QCA/DfES (2003) *Speaking, Listening, Learning: working with children in KS1 and 2*, London: QCA/DfES.

QCA (1999) *Teaching Speaking and Listening in Key Stages 1 and 2*, London: QCA.

QCA (2004) *Introducing the Grammar of Talk*, London: QCA (for KS3/4).

Wragg, E.C., Brown, G. (1993) *Explaining*, London: Routledge.

Wider perspectives

Alexander, R.J. (2001) *Culture and Pedagogy: international comparisons in primary education,* Oxford UK and Malden USA: Blackwell (especially chapter 15 'Interaction, time and pace' and the detailed transcript analyses from classrooms in five countries in chapter 16 'Learning discourse', pp 391-528).

Alexander, R.J. (1995) *Versions of Primary Education,* London: Routledge (see especially the transcript examples and analyses in chapter 4 'Task, time and talk', pp 103-219).

Alexander, R.J. (2008) *Essays on Pedagogy,* London: Routledge (this contains the international sequel to this booklet together with chapters setting classroom talk in the wider contexts of pedagogy, curriculum and educational policy for a changing world).

Barnes, D., Todd, F. (1995) *Communication and Learning Revisited,* London: Heinemann.

Bearne, E., Dombey, H., Grainger, T. (ed) (2003) *Classroom Interactions in Literacy,* Milton Keynes: Open University Press.

Black, P., Harrison, C., Lee, C., Marshall, B., Wiliam, D. (2003) *Assessment for Learning: putting it into practice,* Maidenhead: Open University Press.

Bruner, J.S. and Haste, H.E. (ed) (1987) *Making Sense: the child's construction of the world,* London: Routledge.

Cazden, C.B. (2001) *Classroom Discourse: the language of teaching and learning* (second edition), Portsmouth NH: Heinemann.

Coulthard, M. (1992) *Advances in Spoken Discourse Analysis,* London: Routledge.

Daniels, H. (2001) *Vygotsky and Pedagogy,* London: Routledge/Falmer.

Dillon, J.T. (1990) *The Practice of Questioning,* London: Routledge.

Edwards, A.D., Westgate, D.P.G. (1994) *Investigating Classroom Talk,* London: Falmer.

Edwards, D. and Mercer, N. (1987) *Common Knowledge: the development of understanding in the classroom,* London: Routledge.

Grugeon, E., Dawes, L., Smith, C., Hubbard, L. (2005) *Teaching Speaking and Listening in the Primary School* (third edition), London: David Fulton.

Hargreaves, D.H. (2004) *Personalising Learning 2: student voice and assessment for learning*, London: Specialist Schools and Academies Trust.

Hargreaves, D.H. (2005) *Personalising Learning 5: mentoring and coaching, and workforce development*, London: Specialist Schools and Academies Trust.

Holquist, M. (1990) *Dialogism: Bakhtin and his world*, London: Routledge.

Johnson, M. (2004) *Developmental Cognitive Neuroscience* (second edition), Oxford: Blackwell.

Kotulak, R. (1997) *Inside the Brain: revolutionary studies of how the mind works*, Kansas City: Andrews McMeel.

Lindfors, J.W. (1999) *Children's Inquiry: using language to make sense of the world*, New York: Teacher's College Press.

Mercer, N. (2000) *Words and Minds: how we use language to think together*, London: Routledge.

Mercer, N. and Hodgkinson, S. (ed) (2008) *Exploring Talk in Schools*, London: Sage (a collection of papers by leading figures in the classroom talk reform movement, written in honour of Douglas Barnes).

Mortimer, E.F. and Scott, P.H. (2003) *Meaning Making in Secondary Science Classrooms*, Buckingham: Open University Press.

Myhill, D., Jones, S., Hopper, R. (2005) *Talking, Listening, Learning: effective talk in the primary classroom*, Maidenhead: Open University Press.

Norman, K. (ed) (1992) *Thinking Voices: the work of the National Oracy Project*, London: Hodder.

Nystrand, M. with Gamoran, A., Kachur, R. and Prendergast, C. (1997) *Opening Dialogue: understanding the dynamics of language and learning in the English classroom*, New York: Teachers College Press.

QCA (2003) *New Perspectives on Spoken English in the Classroom:* discussion papers, London: QCA.

Sims, E. (2006) *Deep Learning - 1,* London: Specialist Schools and Academies Trust. (Places dialogic teaching in the context of student voice, metacognition and learning to learn as part of the wider theory of education and pedagogy developed by David Hargreaves (above).

Wells, G. (1999) *Dialogic Enquiry: towards a sociocultural practice and theory of education,* Cambridge: Cambridge University Press.

Wood, D. (1998) *How Children Think and Learn* (second edition), Oxford: Blackwell (especially chapter 6, 'Making sense' and chapter 7 'The literate mind', pp 144-224).

Dialogue, voice, talk for learning and teaching, and the Cambridge Primary Review.

The Cambridge Primary Review, an independent enquiry into the condition and future of primary education in England, takes up many of the themes explored in this booklet.

The Review's final report was published in October 2009. The evidence on which it draws includes official data, written submissions, focus group meetings and surveys of published research commissioned from leading academics. Originally published in stages during 2007-8, the latter now appear in revised form in a companion volume.

Relevant chapters from the two books are as follows:

Alexander, R.J. (ed) (2009) *Children, their World, their Education: final report and recommendations of the Cambridge Primary Review,* Abingdon, Routledge,

chapter 7, 'Children's development and learning'
chapter 10, 'Children's voices'
chapter 11, 'Foundations: the early years'
chapter 12, 'What is primary education for?'
chapter 14, 'Towards a new curriculum'
chapter 15, 'Re-thinking pedagogy'
chapter 16, 'Assessment, learning and accountability'.

Alexander, R.J. with Doddington, C., Gray, J., Hargreaves, L. and Kershner, R. (eds) (2009) *The Cambridge Primary Review Research Surveys*, Abingdon, Routledge,

chapter 2, 'Children and their primary schools: pupils' voices' (Robinson and Fielding)
chapter 6, 'Children's cognitive development and learning' (Goswami and Bryant)
chapter 7, 'Children's social development, peer interaction and classroom learning' (Howe and Mercer)
chapter 19, 'The quality of learning: assessment alternatives for primary education' (Harlen)
chapter 20, 'Learning and teaching in primary schools: insights from TLRP' (James and Pollard)
chapter 29, 'The trajectory and impact of national reform: curriculum and assessment in English primary schools' (Wyse, McCreery and Torrance).

Short summaries of each of the research surveys, though not the surveys in full, may be downloaded from the Review website:
www.primaryreview.org.uk. Also relevant is the report on the Review's 'community soundings' – 87 meetings in nine regional locations through which children, teachers, parents and community representatives expressed their hopes and fears about childhood, education, society and the wider world:

Alexander, R.J. and Hargreaves, L. (2007) *Community Soundings: the Cambridge Primary Review regional witness sessions*, Cambridge: University of Cambridge Faculty of Education,
http://www.primaryreview.org.uk/Downloads/Int_Reps/1.Com_Sdg/Primary_Review_Community_Soundings_report.pdf.